"A solid contribution to ship in the fire service. Larson takes us through confrontations of getting things done in an Emergency Services Department, and you can feel the rewards of hard and thoughtful work in managing toward specific goals."

–Dennis Smith, Author of *San Francisco Is Burning: The Untold Story of the 1906 Earthquake and Fires*

"*Frontline Heroes* is a compelling story with a message that reinforces the difference each of us can make. Each chapter provides guidance on creating an environment that captures the energy and enthusiasm of every person."

–Pam Bilbrey, Author of *Reflections on Leadership: Rants, Raves and Realities* as well as her explosive new hit, *Ordinary Greatness: It's Where You Least Expect It…Everywhere*

"Wow, *Frontline Heroes: A Story of Saving Lives* is a must-read for the modern-day fire/EMS officer. Whether you have been in your position for twenty years, or are aspiring to become a leader in your organization, this book has a message for you. Larson is able to get his message across loud and clear in a very interesting and informative way that will keep you turning pages. If you are interested in being a leader or in sharpening your existing skill set, you will want to own a copy of Kurt Larson's book. This is a must-have addition to every fire/EMS officer's library."

–Dennis Rubin, Fire Chief, District of Columbia Fire Department

"I have had the fortune of teaching with, and learning from, Kurt Larson for many years. In *Frontline Heroes*, Chief Larson perfectly translates our lives to the page. This is a must-read, from rookie to chief."

–Ginny Cranor, Lieutenant/Paramedic, City of Pensacola Fire Department

Frontline Heroes

A Story of Saving Lives

Kurt Larson

Copyright © 2010 Studer Group, LLC

All rights reserved.

Published by:
Fire Starter Publishing
913 Gulf Breeze Parkway, Suite 6
Gulf Breeze, FL 32561
Phone: 850-934-1099
Fax: 850-934-1384
www.firestarterpublishing.com

ISBN: 978-0-9840794-5-2

Library of Congress Control Number: 2009938592

All rights reserved. No part of this book may be used or reproduced in any form or by any means, or stored in a database or retrieval system without the prior written permission of the publisher, except in the case of brief quotations embodied in critical articles or reviews. Making copies of any part of this book for any purpose other than your own personal use is a violation of United States copyright laws. Entering any of the contents into a computer for mailing list or database purposes is strictly prohibited unless written authorization is obtained from Fire Starter Publishing.

Printed in the United States of America

To the Frank Benjamins everywhere, here is our chance to make a difference. One person at a time.

Frontline Heroes:
A Story of Saving Lives

Table of Contents

Foreword i

Introduction v

Prologue: On the Job ix
    The Scene
    More Victims
    The Next Morning

Chapter One: Officer Orientation 1
    Several Weeks Later
    The Boss
    A Dream Job
    The Boardroom
    The Fire Chief Takes Center Stage

Chapter Two: Orientation Continues 13
    The Red Folder
    Fire Prevention
    Test Time
    The Blue and Green Folders
    The Journey Folder

Chapter Three: The Healthcare Flywheel Comes to Life 25
    More Questions Than Answers
    The Morning Meeting
    The Flywheel Explained
    Creating a Great Place to Work
    Back on Duty
    The Bombshell

Chapter Four: What Makes the Flywheel Turn 41
    Values and Passion
    Chief Black Makes Her Rounds
    Letting It Sink In
    Tactical Considerations

Chapter Five: Purpose, Worthwhile Work, Making a Difference . . . 55
    The Reunion
    Reporting for Duty
    Interview with the Battalion Chief
    Engine 15 Responds
    The Business Side of Firefighting
    Meaningful Purpose

Chapter Six: The Flywheel's Principles 69
    A Walking Encyclopedia
    The Prescriptive To-Dos
    Tactical Considerations

Chapter Seven: Commit to Excellence 77
    The Training Center
    Stormy's Story
    The Department's Greatest Asset
    The First Principle
    Tactical Considerations

Chapter Eight: Measurement and Culture 89
    The Important Things
    Focus on Service
    The Construction Crew
    Teamwork Defined
    Tactical Considerations

Chapter Nine: A Chance to Practice 101
    "Respond to an Accident with Injuries"
    Simple Triage and Rapid Treatment
    Medical Officer Duties

Chapter Ten: Creating Leaders and Accountability 111
    Where People Want to Work
    Leadership Investment
    Concentrate on Employees
    Renters Versus Owners
    A Peer Interview in Process
    How It All Fits Together
    Tactical Considerations

Chapter Eleven: Not a False Alarm 125
    Smoke in the Hallways
    The Room on Fire
    A Casualty
    Midnight
    In the Kitchen

Chapter Twelve: Retaining the Best 135
    Leader Accountability
    The Behaviors
    Bright Ideas
    Tactical Considerations

Chapter Thirteen: Alignment, Communication, and Recognition .. 145
    Behaviors in Line with Goals and Values
    Communicate, Communicate, Communicate
    The Power of Storytelling
    Tactical Considerations

Chapter Fourteen: Countdown to Celebration 159
    Lunch with Maggie and Pete
    Call to Sandy
    Sharing with Lexi
    It Takes Courage
    Tactical Considerations

Chapter Fifteen: New Officer Orientation Winds Down 175
    Last-Minute Jitters
    The Three Musketeers, Reunited
    Leading the Way
    A First-Class Reception
    The Banquet
    The Fire Chief Inspires
    Presentation of the Badges

Epilogue 193
    In Front of the Class
    New Officers Celebrate

Acknowledgments 199

Resources 201

About the Author 207

FOREWORD

When many people think of first responders, they think of the heroic characters from television. I understand. I also remember the early TV shows like *Emergency!* For me, first responders are heroes on a personal level. Back in 1995, they saved my son's life.

It was July and my family was camping. My eight-year-old son, Michael, ran to get a soccer ball. Seeing that he was headed for danger, my wife yelled for him to stop. We don't know if Michael didn't hear her or if he was just too focused on getting his soccer ball. What we do know is when he bent down to pick up the ball, a 4,500-pound Bobcat tractor backed up and crushed him.

It's hard to describe that terrible moment. I remember my daughter yelling, "My brother's dead!" I remember my wife bending over Michael and saying, "There's no heartbeat."

Time seemed to freeze—until the ambulance pulled in and two paramedics started working on my son. They were able to restart his heart and move him to the ambulance.

At the first hospital, the emergency room physician decided it would be best to transfer Michael to a larger hospital with a pediatric intensive care unit in a bigger city. My wife rode with him in the ambulance. She reported that as a paramedic tended to my son's body, he also touched her heart.

Eight days later when Michael left the hospital, we thanked the doctors, nurses, respiratory therapists, aides, and all staff with whom we had come into contact.

Even then, we did not go directly home. We drove the 90 minutes back to the scene of the accident and stopped by the firehouse to thank the crew for saving our son's life.

So often, the hospital people get the thanks. I am glad that they do. But for many first responders, it is just back to work to help another person after a patient leaves their care.

Michael made a full recovery in about 18 months. But it was the short amount of time he spent with first responders—time that is probably measured in minutes—that made that recovery possible at all.

When I speak of people who have passion for their work, I am usually speaking of hospital staff. They are my primary audience and I have great admiration for them. But first responders take passion to a whole new level.

In fact, when I hear a complaint about hours, conditions, pay, or benefits, I relay a number of stories about first responders. I then ask the group if first responders make a difference. All heads nod "yes."

I then ask why first responders continue to do their jobs. Is it the hours? The pay? The benefits? Of course, the audience knows that none of these answers is correct. Many times, the people I'm speaking to have jobs with better pay and benefits, and even more of them work normal hours.

We can learn so much from first responders, I tell them. Every time, the audience agrees.

First responders have difference making in their DNA. They are driven by passion. They are intense students because they always want to get better at what they do. After all, lives depend on it.

I first met Kurt Larson, the author of this book, some years ago when he attended one of my two-day conferences called "Taking You and Your Organization to the Next Level." When I speak, there are always a few people who stand out because of their avid listening, note taking, and questions. Kurt is one of those people.

Foreword

Over the years, our paths continued to cross as Kurt persisted in learning and implementing ways to improve first responder organizations as well as his own skill set. Just last week, a volunteer member of a fire department in South Carolina wrote to me after hearing Kurt speak to comment on his passion and the way he connected her back to her own values in making a difference.

While he would if he could, there is no way Kurt could physically carry his message and touch all the people who could benefit from his teachings. So to supplement his travel, he has written a book that will carry the message to others. As many great books do, *Frontline Heroes* uses a story format to impart lessons for work and for home.

I am grateful that Kurt entered my life, and I am honored to write the foreword to his book. Kurt is a difference maker for all the right reasons. If you are taking time to read this book, so are you.

Thank you for being there first.

Quint Studer

INTRODUCTION

Every book shares a message. To me, the message of this book is the journey. While written through the eyes of just one individual, it represents the daily challenges faced by those brave souls who respond every day to the call for help. In the working lives of the firefighters, emergency medical technicians, paramedics, police officers, and chiefs of the world, there are many similarities. One of those similarities is that they never know what to expect, but practically without fail, they're willing to put their lives on the line to save the lives of others.

This book is designed for emergency responders in need of something more than a textbook to teach them management principles. It is meant to help them make a difference in the way they serve their communities, and in turn, help them advance their careers.

During the time I spent training to be a firefighter and later holding leadership positions within departments, the textbooks I read delivered powerful messages, but getting through them was tough. The books did a great job of presenting the material I needed to know, but I've always found that it's much easier and more pleasurable to read a *story* with characters you care about than a book about tactics. That's why I decided to write this book: to provide you with the principles you need in order to be a better leader within the context of an easy-to-read story about someone who is very much like you or someone you know.

What follows is a story of discovery. The chapters present principles that are easy to apply to everyday emergency service operations. Yet, this story depends heavily upon you, the reader, to view it through the eyes of the main character—firefighter and paramedic Frank Benjamin.

Whether you're in a leadership position or working in the trenches, the principles explained throughout this book will help you. If you are a leader, you might find that too often you depend upon simply what is put in the standard operating guidelines and forget about applying management principles in daily operations. The tactics and techniques detailed herein will help you function well day-to-day, just as you already do in a response situation.

Emergency service providers are a rare breed—our lives rarely look the same from one day to the next—and that's why the book is written as it is. It follows a few days in the life of Frank Benjamin, who is a firefighter/paramedic. Don't worry if you're not a firefighter or a paramedic. The principles presented in this book can apply to any first responder, no matter your field. The references to a team-oriented management style and the management principles covered can be practiced by all.

Early in my career I learned three very important lessons. First, emergency services personnel must constantly INNOVATE, ADAPT, and OVERCOME. No one will be there for us except our fellow first responders who have received the same training and have the same love of the job. Second, when people call for help, they're having a bad day. They don't call because the sun rose as usual and the sky is blue—something has gone wrong in their worlds. As first responders, we need to have the skills to handle each and every emergency—simple and complex, routine and "career" calls. Third, it's those things we do when we don't have calls that create a great organization.

So sit back and enjoy. Put yourself in Frank Benjamin's shoes. The book is fast-paced, often rapidly switching from one situation to another, just like our lives. Yes, our days are calm one second and hectic the next, as we rush to help those in our communities. Our minds and bodies jump from one skill or practice we've been trained to perform to the next, in order to save a life or to keep a building from imminent disaster.

Keep in mind, you may find errors in Frank's judgment or in his tactics. It would be easy to write a book with the perfect individual. But would it be real, and could anyone learn from it?

I have a passion to add value to the lives of those who provide service to their communities. Few things are more rewarding to me than to aid first responders and to help them help others. For some, being a first responder is a calling; for others, it's just a job. If you are one of the passionate ones, use your passion to fire up your career. It's what will set you apart from the rest.

With that in mind, I present Frank Benjamin's story.

PROLOGUE

ON THE JOB

You could feel the tension in the cab. The shrill pitch of the siren was rising and falling to encourage traffic ahead of us to quickly move out of the way. Strobe flashes bounced off every surface of the truck. I looked over at Jason, who sat next to me in the cab of the fire engine. We have the seats directly behind the driver and officer, so we see everything backwards. Fully geared up, Jason was busy checking his air pack for any last-minute adjustments. No one knew what to expect.

Five minutes before, we had been sitting in the dayroom listening to the battalion chief tell us what was happening around the department. Then, the weather quickly changed from slightly overcast to a torrential downpour. Before anyone could say anything about the weather situation, we heard what sounded like a train approaching the firehouse. As if in competition with the fury of the rain, alarm tones immediately went out to all the stations to lock down the bay doors and move everyone to an interior room away from windows.

I hadn't entirely put it together yet, but as instructed, I moved with the crowd into the locker room. There were jokes and laughter as we jostled for our own space in the small room. Unsure whether this was just a drill, many of us snapped open our cell phones. Then I heard someone say, "Strange, we've never had a tornado here in our history. Are you sure that's what's happening?"

Frontline Heroes: A Story of Saving Lives

A tornado? *He's joking!* I thought. I wanted to get to a window and see for myself. But before I could, alert tones went off again.

"Tornado on the ground in the area of Main and Jackson. Repeating…"

"Main and Jackson? That's just five blocks away," someone commented.

I still couldn't believe my ears. A tornado? Here? We had been training for years on terrorism, structure fires, and storms of all sorts, but I never expected a tornado. My mind raced. *What should I prepare for?* Before I could answer my own question, the alert tones went off again. This time, they were the tones specific to our station—the ones calling us to duty when those in our community needed us.

"Engine 4, Rescue 2, Respond to a tornado touchdown in the area of Main and Jackson. Time: 12:16."

We all moved quickly to the fire engine. In fact, I hadn't seen anyone move that fast in a long time. Within seconds we were dressed in our bunker gear, scrambling into our seats, and on our way. My adrenalin was pumping so fast I felt like my heart was going to jump straight out of my chest.

I looked back over at Jason. I could tell that his nerves were getting to him, too.

Lieutenant Parker opened the window between the front and back of the fire engine. He yelled to be heard over the whine of the siren and the noise of the engine, giving us our instructions: "Be prepared for anything! Benjamin, you take the lead on patients! McCall, you check for structural stability!"

Again, alert tones were sounding.

"Engine 1, Engine 2, Truck 1, Battalion 1. Respond to a tornado touchdown at the Crossroads Mall. Time: 12:18. Reports coming in of partial roof collapse, cars turned over, and debris through windows."

More alert tones.

"Engine 3, Rescue 1, Truck 2, Battalion 2. Respond to the airport. Commercial aircraft on the runway with flameout and 200 souls on board. Reports of small aircraft strewn across runways and taxiways.

Prologue: On the Job

Terminal reports partial roof removal, overturned cars, and broken windows."

The department was splitting in all directions, news that only made me more apprehensive. We had traveled only about one block and were already slowing down. I knew we couldn't be on scene already, so I craned my neck around to look out the front windshield. All I could see was a view that looked like it was straight out of a war scene in an old movie. Dust in the air, debris everywhere. I yanked off my seat belt, turned around, and knelt on my seat to get a better view. It really looked like a bomb had gone off. There were small fires in cars. Buildings that had been standing proudly just minutes ago were now reduced to piles of rubble.

If this was the beginning of the storm's destructive path, I wondered how far this level of devastation stretched. What would those fire engines responding to areas three to four miles away find?

Without turning to see if we were paying attention, the lieutenant continued, "This is as far as we go. We walk the rest of the way."

Jason and I hopped down from the fire truck as we heard the air brake engage. I snatched the medical kit from the compartment as he grabbed some tools and a fire extinguisher. Then I heard on the truck radio, "Engine 4 on scene at Main and Belmont. Engine 4 will be Belmont Command. We have heavy damage to multiple structures, minor car fires. Beginning search and rescue. Belmont Command will be changing to Tactical Channel 2."

I changed the portable radio I was carrying to TAC 2. Then, "Belmont Command, Rescue 2," a voice crackled.

"This is Belmont Command," Lieutenant Parker answered.

"We are unable to reach your location. We have multiple patients with moderate injuries who can be treated on scene. Recommend you send patients to our location as a treatment and transportation area. We are at Belmont and Graham."

"Understood, set up treatment and transportation at Belmont and Graham."

I had heard that disaster rescues of this nature turned into organized chaos. It looked like that would be the case for us that day as Rescue 2 could not reach our location and had to improvise.

The Scene

As I looked up the hill ahead of me, trees stood at odd angles without any leaves. Branches were broken, twisted, and mangled. Insulation hung from limbs along with clothing, furniture, and even a large television set. Where there were fences, debris was pushed into the chain link, and in some places it looked like someone had tried to push something through without caring that the item was too big to fit in such a tiny opening.

Jason and I walked up the street. People were just now beginning to appear. We were in a residential area of town. It was a Thursday afternoon, and I hoped most people were still at work.

The first house we came to was standing straight and tall. Some of its windows were broken, but otherwise it looked all right. We banged on the door. Nobody answered. We looked in every window we could. Since we didn't see or hear anything, we sprayed an X on the door, noting the date, time, and our call sign, and continued on.

Next, we came to a quaint little red house that turned out to be a daycare center for a local church. Not a single window was spared on the side where we stood. We banged on the door. A lady in her late 50s opened the door, pushing aside broken glass underfoot.

"Oh," she screamed. "Thank heaven! We have about 20 babies here. They're okay, but scared. We moved everyone to the bathroom. Please. Please. Come with me."

She hustled down a narrow, darkened hallway looking back over her shoulder at us as if to urge us to move faster. We radioed a short report and raced after her.

It felt like it took an eternity to travel the short hallway. The second door on the right was open just a crack with a little light glowing

Prologue: On the Job

around the frame. The lady pushed the door open, and we could hear muted crying and singing.

As we reached the door ourselves, I peered around it and nearly did a double take. Jason leaned around me to take a look for himself. There were two young ladies in the bathtub with about 10 infants sitting on them and between them. They were singing lullabies to the kids to keep them calm. A single small candle in the sink lit up the room. One lady's face was ashen, and she appeared visibly shaken. But she kept singing to calm the infants. I don't think I'll ever forget that image.

"Ladies, we're with the fire department. How can we help?" I asked as I looked around the tiny bathroom. I don't think we could have squeezed another living being into that room. It measured five by eight feet, with the bathtub against the outside wall. With Jason and me, the two women in the bathtub, 10 infants, the lady who had brought us into the room, and all the bath fixtures, it was a tight fit, to say the least.

"Oh, young man, can you take these babies to a safe place?" asked one of the women in the bathtub.

"How many children do you have here? Are there any injuries? We can stay here until additional help arrives, but I need to know if anyone is hurt."

She looked up at me with pleading eyes and said, "They're okay. We can stay a little longer if we must. How're the others?"

"Others?" Jason replied.

"Yes, there are three more women and about 10 kids. Last time I saw them, they were in the toddler room."

I looked at the woman who brought us to this point as she opened her mouth and gasped. "I was so worried about the babies I nearly forgot about them…they're so quiet and all."

She pushed past us before I could even respond, dashed down the hallway, and disappeared around the corner.

More Victims

Jason took off after her while I hung back to radio in a report and ask for backup. Still talking, I started off in pursuit of Jason and nearly ran into him as I rounded the corner. Our guide was frantically yanking on the doorknob and trying to gain entry without success. Jason attempted to move her aside, but she didn't budge.

Finally he nearly shouted, "Excuse me, ma'am, let me try!"

Startled, she moved aside. To make it easier for us to work, I pulled the woman behind me. Not only was she out of the way, she was also out of view of the doorway.

Jason put his shoulder against the door, turned the handle and shoved. It didn't move. Since Jason is 6'2", 220 pounds, I was surprised. Even if the door was out of plumb, it should have budged. He put his face to the door and said, "If you can hear me, stand away from the door!"

He tried the door handle one more time to see if it would open on its own. Nothing. Jason lifted his Halligan to just above the latch, placed the fork into the jamb, and pulled backwards. The door gave a little. He placed the fork a little further in and pulled again. The door gave a little more. Enough that we could now see into the room.

Insulation was everywhere. The ceiling had fallen in. The air was thick with dust, and although we could see fairly well, it was like looking through a dense fog. Mounds of drywall were randomly scattered under the insulation, and all the windows were blown out. Pictures and posters were torn from the walls, yet a few decorations dangled precariously by what seemed like a thread. Jason yelled into the room, "Fire department, anyone in here?"

Our guide was frantic to see inside. For a second, I thought she might climb right over me to get a look.

We listened intently for a response. My heart thumped loudly as I awaited an answer. I felt a trickle of sweat slide down the middle of my back. I had trained for this type of situation, but never really thought about how I would feel the first time I experienced it face to face. With the windows broken out throughout the building, all we could hear was the wind, rain, and sirens. Not a sound came from the room—until finally, what looked like a hand appeared from a debris pile in the far corner of the room and we heard a faint, "Over here."

Jason and I pushed in unison against the blocked door. No luck. Jason squeezed the Halligan through the small opening and slowly swept debris from behind the door. We pushed again, and made a little headway. Frantically, our guide pushed in behind us. I understood her urgency, but safety was our first priority.

As I moved her back a little, I said, "Ma'am, please let us go to them and hand them to you in the doorway. It'll be safer for you and the kids."

"Okay, okay, I'm just so concerned."

As Jason continued to push open the door inch by inch, I reflected on how amazing it was to see these women caring so diligently for the kids. They understood the magnitude of the danger they were in, yet had been singing to the children to keep them calm. I knew that took a lot of nerve—to stay composed in the midst of such chaos.

"It'll be all right," I assured her.

I looked back to my partner. Jason had pushed through the small opening and was beginning to methodically dig through the debris. Out of the corner of my eye, I saw what looked like the edge of a mattress. Then a shoe. Again, cautioning our guide to stay outside the room, I barreled through the doorway. My breathing mask got hooked on the doorknob, and I was jerked backwards. *Calm down*, I told myself and sheepishly unhooked it. I waded through the mess and helped Jason with his task. Soon, the mattress was cleared enough to lift it off of whatever was below.

I picked up a corner, and Jason did the same with the opposing corner. We heaved the mattress toward the wall. A huge plume of dirt and dust rained down on us, blocking our view. Even through my goggles, I could feel grit in my eyes. Holding my breath, I waited for the air to clear. A woman, covered with dust and dirt, and with a bloody cut above her left eye, sat up and coughed. She was surrounded by four pairs of shiny eyes peering out from small dirt-covered faces. Not one of them was crying, but you could see the leftover streaks from tears shed at some point during their treacherous experience. They were all small. The oldest couldn't have been more than five, and the youngest looked to be about three. I noticed a few cuts and abrasions, but everyone was breathing. The bleeding, I knew, could be controlled with small bandages. Thankfully, no one appeared to be seriously injured.

In a hoarse voice, the woman said, "We're okay, but Ginger was on the other side…over there."

She waved her hand to the far side of the room where there was another pile of debris about three feet tall. Insulation, drywall, and a rocking chair lay on top of a second king size mattress. However, we had to get these kids out of the way before we could do anything for the others.

After a quick triage, I helped the woman to her feet. Jason remained with the children as I shuffled a path through the muck and handed the woman off to our escort outside the door. They hugged and laughed and carried on like they hadn't seen each other in years. I can't even imagine what they were thinking while the daycare building caved in around them.

Leaving them at the door, I trudged back to the four children. I wanted to carry two and have Jason do the same, but there were still a multitude of obstacles in the way, and I didn't want to fall. It seemed like an eternity while we carried the children to safety. I thought about splitting up and having Jason start on the pile where the other victims might be, but safety won out.

Jason and I worked to unbury what we suspected were the other kids and Ginger. The further we dug, the more debris there seemed to be. Finally we got down to the level of the mattress. As we lifted it, we heard cheering. We threw the mattress in the area recently vacated by the last set of kids. When we looked back, a dusty blanket was being pulled down, exposing a large wooden table. Under the table were six smiling kids and two grown women.

"See, we told you the firefighters would be here soon!" said one of them. "Now, listen to me. Miss Jenny and I want you to follow your

Prologue: On the Job

fire drill and go to the meeting place. And if the firefighters tell you to do something, do it."

She handed each of us a child who, in turn, we handed off to one of the other ladies. It was like a bucket brigade, except we were handing off children in place of water. Then, we helped Ginger and Jenny to their feet.

"Is there anyone else?" I asked.

"Just the babies," Jenny told us. "They're in the bathroom. Safest place to put them."

"They were okay," I replied. "Can you two walk out?"

"Sure, if we can get over this stuff," Ginger said as she swept her hand through the air, gesturing at all the devastation.

We helped them get to the door. When we got to the hallway, not a child was in sight.

"Hey, where'd everyone go?" Jason asked.

"They're out at our designated emergency meeting place, the mailbox," Ginger responded.

We followed the ladies out, and on our way, checked to make sure the rest of the building was empty.

"Belmont Command, Engine 4 portable."

"Engine 4 portable, go ahead."

"We are up the hill at the second building. We need assistance. Have at least ten children, ten infants, and five adults who were trapped in a structure. We need additional personnel to transport the children to the treatment area."

"Command copies, need personnel to transport children to treatment."

I looked over to Jason and the ladies at the mailbox. He was talking quietly to the workers, who had children surrounding them, clinging to their waists as if trying to climb up trees. As for the babies, there they were, neatly lying in a row on a blanket someone had provided for them.

"Help is on the way," I told the assembled group. "Let's see what we have here while we wait."

Jason began handing me one child at a time to examine as he continued to do what he could to calm everyone down. In short order we had thoroughly examined each of the kids. Through all the turmoil, there were only a few minor cuts, which we covered with bandages. As we finished with the last child, it began to rain again. Fortunately, the crew from Engine 6 was available to help get everyone to a safer location.

As I painted the X on the wall to indicate primary search completed, the radio crackled to life.

"Belmont Command, Engine 6. Have met up with Engine 4 crew and will be taking a group to the church on corner of Main and Breeze set up as the evac area. Paramedic advises only minor injuries. Can handle treatment at this location and release to families."

I looked up ahead to a church down the street. It was like watching the town's annual parade, which always included some of us firefighters walking in full gear. This time, though, each firefighter had a baby in each arm. Jason had a single file line of kids behind him, each holding the hand of the child behind, just as they had been taught. The ladies helped each other along, holding umbrellas over the heads of the line of children and firefighters.

When we arrived at the church, we were met by an emergency medical services (EMS) unit, police officers, and the media. Fortunately for us, we were able to hand over everyone to EMS and return to our search and rescue duties.

The rest of the afternoon we spent searching for victims, stabilizing areas where we could, and putting out small fires. All in all, we were very lucky that the storm passed through when it did. As I had hoped, many of the homes were empty because people were at work. Although there was a large amount of destruction, there was only one serious injury, which had been caused by a beam hitting an elderly gentleman in the head. Over 30 homes had been destroyed, and many more residences and small businesses had been damaged.

Lieutenant Parker did a great job managing the chaos. I vowed that whenever I had the opportunity to lead, I would follow his calming example. He was prepared for the worst disaster and had equipped us to be our most effective. He said to Jason and me, "Great job, guys. You performed well today."

Little did he know how much that meant to us.

When we returned to quarters at about 5:30 p.m., we were wiped out. Dinner never tasted so good, nor was my chair ever so comfortable. As I ate, I hoped that we wouldn't get a call that night.

The Next Morning

Where am I? I wondered as I groggily opened my eyes. I felt like I had been squeezed through a grinder. Even the bones in my fingers were sore. Then it all flooded back to me. The tornado. The rescue and exhaustion that followed it. The pride I had felt for my lieutenant and my team. I slowly flexed each major muscle to see if I was going to be able to get out of bed without groaning. My mind reflected on the scenes from the day before.

Why did things come together so well? I wondered. *Was it purely our training, the skills of my lieutenant, or some other factors I didn't even know about yet?*

As I ate breakfast, I thought about what the weeks ahead held for me and my future as a first responder. I had passed the promotional exam and would be attending orientation soon. I was excited, but also extremely nervous about what the new leadership position would bring. *Could I be as great as the lieutenant?*

Meanwhile, I knew I had a job to do…to be the best firefighter and paramedic I could be. I was looking forward to the new challenge, knowing I could make a difference in the quality of service I provided. I rolled out of bed and hit the floor running. I had work to do before the oncoming shift came in.

CHAPTER ONE

OFFICER ORIENTATION

Several Weeks Later

It was 6:30 a.m. on Monday morning, and it was unusual for me to be at the headquarters office this early. However, with my wife on a business trip and the fact that it was orientation day for my new job as lieutenant, getting to the office early just seemed like the thing to do. I didn't expect to see anyone, yet when I arrived, there was one car already in the parking lot. The gold leaf lettering on its side indicated that it belonged to the emergency medical service (EMS) chief, my new boss. I hadn't really gotten to know the chief and wondered why she was at the office so early. We kidded around a lot in our group of firefighters that it was likely the chief worked bankers' hours.

I had just recently received a promotion from paramedic to lieutenant. Usually, I reported for duty at a firehouse as a member of a four-person team. But because of the promotion, that Monday I reported to the administrative offices for the famous—or infamous, I should say—mandatory, one-day orientation.

We had all heard about orientation. Co-workers had told me that it was simply a formality and that I shouldn't worry about it, that I already knew everything I needed to know. They told me that my higher-ups would hand me my badge, shake my hand, give me a copy of the standard operating procedure manual and my own portable radio, and then I'd be on my way.

With reluctance, I prepared myself to smile, shake hands, and get through it. *Was this really all getting promoted was good for?* I had definitely seen some action before my promotion. I'd been part of one of the busiest houses in the city. As a paramedic assigned to an engine company, I ran not only EMS calls, but went to fires as well. I'd been to little house fires and major commercial fires. And then there were times when the patients themselves could cause you more harm than the fires. You never know what someone will do, or where someone is hiding when you are on their turf.

I reached for the handle of the administration building's front door. Through the glass, I could see that there weren't any lights on in the offices. *Stay calm*, I reminded myself. *Why are you so nervous?* Everyone told me there was nothing to worry about, and that I should just have fun. Besides, they all said that no matter what, I already had the job.

I willed myself to project an air of casualness, grabbed the door handle, and prepared to strut into the building. However, I nearly slammed into the still-locked door. Well, I guess that made sense. It was 6:30 a.m., after all. The building was dark, so why would I expect the door to be unlocked? I furtively glanced around. The chief's car was still the only one in the lot. *Did she leave it overnight, or is she inside the building already?* Thoughts raced through my mind. I didn't want to appear uncertain or just plain stupid—I hoped no one had seen me try to open the front door. I just couldn't seem to shake my orientation day nerves.

I decided that perhaps I should try to find an open door or return to my car. I walked around the side of the building. The headquarters is a two-story brick office building with a curved atrium and floor-to-ceiling windows. An attractive sidewalk skirted the building with a strip of grass between it and headquarters, and continued to the other side of the yard next to the parking area. The flowers and shrubbery added a nice touch.

Chapter 1: Officer Orientation

As I wandered around the building, I saw a light on the first floor near the side entrance. *Would I startle the person inside by arriving so early?* I wondered. I decided to give the door a try. It opened, so I knew someone expected others to come through that door. I peeked into the building and listened. I didn't hear a thing. No shuffling of papers, no copier clanking a tune, not even the air conditioner's low hum. "Anyone here?" I called.

"Back here," came the reply.

The Boss

Chief Elle Black was sitting at a table in the break room with a steaming beverage in her hand. She was the division chief in charge of emergency medical operations for the fire department. Chief Black had started out with the department as a firefighter. As the fire service progressed and embraced providing emergency medical services, her skills took her up the promotional ladder, eventually to division chief—managing the Emergency Medical Service (EMS) program. This was quite an accomplishment. Not only was EMS relatively new to the fire service, so were women.

In the fire service, most female members don't have time to care about appearances. This didn't seem to be the case for Chief Black. At just 5'6" and attractive with shoulder-length hazel brown hair, she appeared quite trim. And she had an undeniably commanding presence. She looked to be in her mid-thirties, yet I knew she was a decade older than that. It was well known that she believed physical fitness was important to maintaining not only fire service readiness, but one's own personal health as well. Perhaps that's what helped her look so young?

Several times during her training classes, she had quoted an article by Stefanos Kales of the Harvard School of Public Health. It said that firefighters' sudden intense physical exertion and exposure to heat, along with the chemicals and smoke they breathe in, can put enough stress on the heart to spark a heart attack. She had been promoting lifestyle changes within the department for a while. In fact, she was the first to cite for our department that 45 percent of on-duty deaths can be attributed to heart attacks. Now she had scientific evidence to support her belief.

Her mission was to promote healthy work and home environments. A philosophy new to the department, it was met with some resistance. I knew of firefighters who would say as she walked into a room, "Put the donuts away, here comes the fitness police."

Some would be intimidated by such actions, but Chief Black had the presence of mind to come back with a good quip like, "If you wanted to be a cop, why didn't you just say so?"

So, regardless of how you felt about her promotion of good health, you had to admit she stood her ground while trying to make our jobs safer.

"My, you're here early," she said, looking up from something she'd been reading.

"I just thought I'd get a jump on the day," I replied, trying to sound casual.

Did she know who I was? I wondered. *Why was she here so early? Had my thoughts about administration and bankers' hours been wrong? What should I do?*

I really didn't have a game plan for what I would do after arriving so early. I thought I could get some brownie points for appearing well before orientation started, but I wasn't at all prepared for a one-on-one with the chief.

I saw that her morning reading consisted of quite a few different materials. Spread out on the table were the city's local paper, the *Wall Street Journal*, a fire service trade journal, several reports, and a coloring book. Naturally, I was curious about the coloring book, but didn't dare ask. Instead, I reached out to shake the chief's hand and said, "Hi. My name is Frank Benjamin."

"It's nice to meet you, Frank," she said. "My name is Elle Black. What brings you to the admin building so early in the morning?"

Chapter 1: Officer Orientation

"I just received a promotion to lieutenant from paramedic. I'm here to attend today's orientation."

"It's good to see people who want to make a difference get promoted," she said. "I imagine you've heard this orientation is a waste of time, but you've entered a new, important phase in your career. Guess you'll have a little time to wait. Would you like a cup of coffee?"

"No thanks, never really acquired the habit," I said.

She poured herself another cup and returned to the table. "Sit down and relax," she said. "I'm sure nobody will be in for about 30 minutes or so. This is normally my quiet time. No kids, no dogs, no husband. Just a little time to think about why I'm here."

A Dream Job

Why I'm here? I wondered what she meant. Of course everybody knew why *she* was there. She was the EMS chief. Her job was to manage our fire service EMS programs, and it was one of the best ones around. It took some babysitting at times, as well as an open mind and vision for change. Yet, I couldn't think of another instance of a department operating its own rescue, ambulance, and pre-hospital care programs seamlessly along with firefighters.

The truth is, it had always been my goal to be a firefighter or paramedic. I was relatively new since I'd only been with the department for five years, but this was my dream job. And I was happy I got to wake up in the morning and go to work at a job through which I could help people, day in and day out. I knew that when folks called us, they were not having a good day. It was my job to make it better, or at least to try to.

I had been lucky as well. My first assignment was with a ladder company. The lieutenant was big-time into training. We trained all the time. Some days we'd come in and the lieutenant, who we called LT, would have us up on the roof learning about how a building was built—from the top down. He said we needed to see the building from another perspective.

LT was also the first person to tell me I had a talent in medicine. He said, "I know this sounds corny, but Johnny Gage and Roy DeSoto got me interested in becoming a firefighter." (Gage and DeSoto were firefighter/paramedic characters from the '70s TV series *Emergency!*)

LT pushed me and assisted with my application for emergency medical technician school, my first real step toward becoming a paramedic.

Even after I got into the EMT class, LT helped get me organized and kept me on task. With everything that goes on in a firehouse, finding time to study was difficult. The guys in the firehouse were great, though. They never complained about me and my studying. In fact, they lent a hand in rearranging some of my duties so that I could study right after dinner.

With LT's help, I graduated at the top of my class. As soon as an opportunity presented itself, I entered the paramedic program and spent close to a year learning how to do my job. Pharmacology, cardiology, and A and P (anatomy and physiology) became my new language. After two years on the ladder truck, I was reassigned to an engine company. I missed the specialized duties we handled on the ladder, but I sure wasn't going to be doing any patient care if I remained there.

Things on the fire engine were different. Now I was responsible for taking care of the patient while others assisted. All eyes were on me, and I had to sink or swim. New location, new challenges. Traditions die hard but the brotherhood survives, and at both firehouses, we worked closely as a strong team. My role was to lead only when a patient was involved. When we went to a fire, I was a follower. I was assigned to a crew fighting fires or searching for victims under the command of the engine company lieutenant.

The next several years flew by. My job was going well, and no two calls were alike. I can't say I was complacent, but it had been awhile since I'd really been challenged. Then one day, out of the blue, the LT from my first ladder company called and said, "Frank, I know you enjoy

Chapter 1: Officer Orientation

your job but I think it's time you started working for a promotion. The lieutenant's test is scheduled, and I want you to sign up and take it."

I took LT's advice, studied, and to my surprise, got a call that I had been selected for promotion. So there I was that morning, sitting in the admin office, rubbing elbows with the EMS chief.

I must have had a strange look on my face because Chief Black asked, "Are you okay?"

Coming back to the moment, I nodded. "Just remembering how I got here," I told her.

"Really," she said. "Tell me about it."

So I relived much of the last five years: my successes, my failures, insecurities…everything. I don't know for sure, but the chief seemed truly interested. I must have talked for about 25 minutes before I said, "This is awfully rude of me," and apologized for monopolizing the conversation.

"Not a problem," she said. "It's good to know who I'm working with."

She stood up, gathered her reading materials, and looked at me. "Now it's my turn to be sorry. I have a conference call to take, and if I'm not mistaken, you have an orientation at 7:30 a.m."

I glanced at my watch and mentally slapped myself on the forehead for not using this time to instead learn more about her.

The Boardroom

It was 7:05 a.m. I walked down the hall in search of the boardroom where orientation would take place. There were more lights on now. The building had a hum to it, with people busy on their computers, coffee machines perking out their tunes, and the air conditioning system waking to its long day's work. What a change. Quiet less than an hour ago, and now crackling with life. I could appreciate why Chief Black came in before the others.

Located off the atrium entrance, the boardroom was nice, though nothing spectacular. Clean. Well organized. At the front was a semi-circular wooden table on a low-rise platform stretching from one side of the room to the other. Behind the table were executive, high backed, leather chairs. A podium stood facing the table and chairs. Beyond it were neat rows of stackable chairs, the kind that make sure you pay attention. No fluff.

Just then a loud whine interrupted my thoughts. A panel descended from the ceiling with an audio-visual projector attached. A small gentleman entered the room. "Oh, I didn't know anyone else was here," he said.

"My name is Frank Benjamin," I replied. "I'm here for the orientation."

"Conrad Zuse," he said. "I'm just here to get the room set up and the materials passed out. Make yourself comfortable."

I watched in fascination as he worked like a conductor over the controls, testing lights, sound, and so forth, putting together his electronic orchestra. After a few minutes he was done. He walked over to me, extending his hand. "Welcome," he said. "I think you're going to enjoy this."

I didn't have the heart to tell him that everyone I talked to said that the orientation was boring. So I just nodded. "Thanks," I said.

Conrad continued setting up the room. Finally, he went out and brought back a box stuffed with folders. The folders were different colors and were grouped by color. Red, blue, green, even purple.

He carefully placed one of each color on the table in front of each of the executive chairs. Then, he placed a small table next to the podium. On it he placed one notebook that had no markings at all. Reaching over to a handle in the wall, Conrad pulled open a small door. Inside was another control center with a small monitor built in. After he flipped a few switches, the monitor came to life. It was a computer control center for presentations. I could now see a DVD player, video player, even a small presentation projector—all integrated into a system.

Chapter 1: Officer Orientation

As I looked up, I could see the image from the monitor gaining clarity on the screen behind the table. It got brighter and brighter until the image on the monitor could be clearly seen without dimming the lights. Conrad looked up and said, "Well, that does it. Best of luck with your new job! If I can be of assistance, please let me know."

And with that he walked out. I noticed several other people entering the room. Since none of them were wearing uniforms—one of our instructions for the day was to wear civilian clothing—I assumed they were there for orientation as well.

As I went over and introduced myself, I was met with handshakes and smiles. Maggie Winters, the only woman in the group, asked, "Is this going to take long? They didn't give a lot of information, just be here at 7:30 a.m., not in uniform. If it's going to be like everyone says, it sounds like we might be in for a waste of time."

"Hi. I'm Pete. Peter Kent. Don't mind her, she's having issues."

With that, Maggie smacked him in the arm. I wondered about their relationship. I later found out that they had been in the same academy and had worked with each other for the last four years. In my book at least, that was enough to qualify them as family. We stood around and talked for a few minutes while others entered and milled around.

The Fire Chief Takes Center Stage

At 7:30 a.m. exactly, the fire chief walked in and said, "Okay, let's get started." The chief seemed different than I remembered him. More confident or calm, something I just couldn't put my finger on. But then again, I'd only met him once when I was hired. At that time, he was in the fire prevention bureau.

Slightly graying at the temples, the chief was in his late forties or early fifties. His uniform sparkled. Well-pressed clothes, shoes shined, brass polished—exactly how I expected a fire chief to look. I had heard that Chief Seale was a stickler for discipline. Perhaps that's why he started on time. Though, it certainly was refreshing not to have to sit around and wait.

As if reading my mind, he said, "I won't waste your time. You're here because you have been selected for promotion. In the past, we have not done you right by simply giving you a badge, a radio, and then just sending you off to the wolves. As of now, we're making changes. I want to take the next several hours to give you an idea of what we expect from you. At the same time, I want to answer your questions and concerns about your job, this department, and how you fit into the big picture. Now if you'll please take your places where your name tags have been placed, we can begin."

We looked at each other. While the chief had been talking, his assistant had been placing name tents on the table. I was seated between Pete and Maggie. What was interesting, however, was that we were sitting at the board table with the screen behind us. The chief was standing at the podium. However, I noticed that a second screen behind the podium, where normally an audience would be sitting, was projecting exactly the same thing as the screen behind the board chairs. This way, board members and the audience could refer to the same presentation without having to turn around. What a great idea!

Once we got settled in, Chief Seale continued.

"In the past, we have made some mistakes. We're going to try and correct some of those mistakes, but we need your input. Today, we'll give you an overview of the organization, our commitment to excellence, our culture, and where we want to go from here. Some of this you may have heard when you first joined the department. Other components will be new to you.

"We're working together to provide the best services possible to the community we protect. So here is what we are going to do…" The chief went on to explain the different speakers from whom we would hear, where they fit into the organization, and how they would impact our abilities to do our jobs.

With the overview laid out, he continued. "For those of you who don't know, I come from a background of dealing with people. In this case, that's you, our newest officer corps. We understand there are certain things you need, want, and desire. One of those is training, so that's why we're here today. Use your own judgment to decide when to get up, stretch, grab some coffee, or whatever. However, we do ask that you be quick about it. Some people have told me that this is the 'chief nitpicking.' Well, it is and it isn't. We are not here to make you uncomfortable. We simply want you at ease, by knowing up-front the 'rules' of the game."

Wow, I thought. *Telling us the rules before the meeting starts? I wonder what we're in for today?*

Chief Seale went on to explain that the colored folders in front of us were not to be opened until we were told to do so, but that their purposes, along with the reasons why we couldn't open them now, would be identified later. As the chief was talking to us, his tone of voice was like that of my father when he was trying to teach me how to ride my bike for the first time without training wheels. Comforting, to the point, and at the same time reassuring.

I found it hard to concentrate on everything Chief Seale said. My mind drifted. *Was I really here, or was this just a great dream?* Trying to focus on the chief, I heard him declare, "We are proud of your accomplishments and of your dedication to this organization as well as to the community. When you put on your uniform every morning, we are proud to have you represent this organization."

He went on to say that the orientation we were about to embark on had not been presented to our department before. We would be taking lessons learned from other organizations that had excelled so that we too could move our organization to the next level. To do that, we would need dedication, persistence, and patience. Chief Seale then asked, "Do each of you have these qualities? If not, your learning curve will be straight uphill."

I looked about the table. Nobody said anything. I guess we were all overwhelmed by what we were hearing. This was not what anyone had told us to expect. Generally, people were silently nodding, smiling back at the chief. Yet, no one spoke or uttered a sound.

CHAPTER TWO

ORIENTATION CONTINUES

The Red Folder

The fire chief continued, "Since I don't see or hear any objections to what I've said, let's dig right in. Please take the red folder and open it."

We all did as instructed. Inside we found an organizational chart of the department, with people's pictures where the names were usually printed. I recognized some of them, but not all.

The chief continued, "Here you have a standard organizational chart. However, we have not added the names or ranks of the individuals pictured. Your job is to find out about the people on page two. In the next week, I want you to find out what each person is all about. Not simply their title or how long they've been with the department. I want you to know who they are."

That should be easy, I thought. I knew most of the pictures on that page. I started scribbling notes. Then Chief Seale said, "This must be completed by next Monday. That gives you a week."

It was then that I heard Maggie grumble under her breath, "One week too long. Let's get it done and over with. What a waste of time."

I put aside the organizational chart. Looking at the materials before me, I wondered what each of them was for. Before I could thumb through everything, the chief's voice broke through my daydreaming.

"Also in your red folder, you will find information on how the fire suppression division works. By that, I mean a current copy of the standard operating guidelines and the state statute that authorizes this organization to provide service to the community. You'll also see a copy of the codes and standards with regard to what you are required to have in the way of licenses, training, continuing education, worker's compensation, work hours, fair labor standards, union activity, and so on. Some of it's for your reference. The people who look to you for leadership will ask you questions, and this will help you provide some of the answers. Remember, we are not trying to make you lawyers. We're only trying to give you an understanding of how the system works. Clear?"

Everyone nodded in agreement. The chief then introduced the fire suppression division chief. With gray hair, he was probably somewhere in his mid- to late fifties. Regardless, he looked like he was ready to step in to save the day should the occasion present itself. He explained to us how the division worked, the different levels that existed, and who the players were. None of this was new, as each of us came from the firehouses. The fire suppression division chief went on to explain how we fit into the big picture, response patterns, communications, and more. Before I realized it, an hour had passed and the division chief was wrapping up his presentation.

There must have been something on our faces, because the fire chief said, "Before we go any further, let's take a break. Coffee is in the break room with some snacks to bring your blood sugar back up."

He didn't know how thankful we were for the breather.

As we walked out, Maggie and Pete were talking. She was saying that she didn't understand why the chief was making such a big deal by having the suppression chief make a presentation. I was about to enter the conversation when Pete exclaimed, "Oh, Maggie, chill out. You're getting paid. The room is air conditioned. The kids aren't bothering you. Besides, now we have some tools to help us. Remember when you were new, and the LT said, 'Just do it because I said so?' Remember how mad you got? And then told me there had to be a reason we do what we do? Remember?"

Maggie must not have expected this from Pete. Her head hung down as she said, "Yeah, I remember. But why does he have to take so long? I have other things I need to be doing. I probably won't even remember half this stuff tomorrow anyway."

"That's okay. At least we have the stuff and can look up things if we need to. We don't want to be lieutenants like the old stick in the mud we had straight out of the academy," said Pete.

I guess I chuckled a little too loudly because Maggie hit me in the arm. "Who you laughin' at?" she asked.

"Hey, I wasn't laughing at you. It's just that I thought the same thing a few years ago about the Neanderthal I had when my LT took a vacation," I said apologetically. And I said to myself, *I'd better keep my distance from her; she's got quite an arm.*

During the break, the group split up into little subgroups. There was Maggie, Pete, and myself, and a group of four guys, each six feet in height or over. There were several more people who were sporting military haircuts, and another group of three. It was like being in high school again, trying to find out where you fit in.

I grabbed a bagel and slathered on some strawberry flavored cream cheese, impressed that they were giving us first-class treatment for our orientation day. As I went to join Pete and Maggie, I heard the chief tell everyone we needed to get back together as we still had a lot to cover.

Fire Prevention

Chief Seale next introduced the fire prevention bureau's chief. We had been told that he was the gatekeeper. If you wanted future promotions, you had to butter up the "old man." Chief Doug Schneider was on his second tour in the fire service. He'd already retired from one agency when he was tapped to develop an interactive organization to meet the needs of our community. Only in his mid-fifties, he was referred to as the "old man" because he had helped so many become good officers.

Chief Schneider was a professional. He knew the ins and outs of the fire service. Best of all, he had unquestionable integrity. He was known for his ability to cut through the fluff and go right to the issue at hand. If you were assigned to the fire prevention bureau, chances were good that someday you would become an officer.

In the prevention bureau, the chief had a system of continuing education. You learned not only about suppression and EMS, but also about human relations. He wanted you to know how to get the community to comply with code issues because they wanted to be safer, not because of a fine or financial impact. He also insisted that his personnel work with response crews on pre-incident planning so that when a fire truck arrived during an emergency, the building was not new to them.

My LT came from a tour in the bureau, and this training paid off for me. From the pre-incident plan, the LT was regularly able to identify the best way to get our critical patients out of a building quickly with little impact on an office environment. The patients never really knew that the LT helped them get paramedic treatment more quickly. He also saved them from the embarrassment of coworkers seeing them at their worst, and from having to answer questions like, "What happened?"

The prevention chief's presentation also took about an hour, but I felt it was not enough time as he had so many good things to tell us. *Who knows?* I thought to myself. *Maybe someday I'll apply for a tour in the fire prevention bureau.* Officers like Chief Schneider were turning that department, once stigmatized as less than optimal for career progress, into a new and improved area. He was upgrading operations in this customer contact area by recruiting the best and brightest to work for him.

I looked down. The red folder was empty. The fire chief was back. Before we could ask any questions, he said, "Ladies and gentlemen, I know you've been sitting a while and need some time to absorb this. Yet, we still have a lot to do, so I'd appreciate it if you can make this a quick lunch. We've set out food for you in the break room. Please grab something to eat, and meet in the courtyard—off limits to anyone but you."

Instantly, all you could hear were papers shuffling and people beginning to move.

Test Time

Again, the food looked terrific. Even Maggie, our resident cynic, said how nice it was. "I can't believe they're treating us like this."

We each grabbed dishes and utensils, filled our plates, and went outside. It was a nice day. The sun was shining, and it was not too hot, not too cold. We made ourselves comfortable and began to eat. About 20 minutes later, the chief came out. "How was lunch?" he asked.

Almost in unison, we all said, "Terrific!"

He smiled. "Sorry this was such a short break from speaker presentations," he said. "I know you need down time. In 10 minutes, I'd like to get started again. We'll begin with a test. See you inside."

You could immediately feel the wind taken out of our sails. *A test*, I thought. *Why are we having a test right now? We haven't even studied.* Everyone became a little more focused than we'd been just moments before. You could feel the change like a weather front moving through.

As we arrived at our seats, there was a page upside down on top of each green folder. Chief Seale said, "Thank you for being so prompt. In front of you is a test. Please do not put your name on it. You're the only one who needs to know what you write. When you finish, turn it over and set aside your pencil so I know you're done."

I looked at the test. On it were several questions with a grading scale from 1 to 10, 1 being the lowest, and 10 being the highest. Each question asked for the test taker's opinion about something. Like so:

Frontline Heroes: A Story of Saving Lives

"How important is it for an organization to strive to go from good to great?"

☐1 ☐2 ☐3 ☐4 ☐5 ☐6 ☐7 ☐8 ☐9 ☐10
_____
_____

"How important is having a commitment to excellence?"

☐1 ☐2 ☐3 ☐4 ☐5 ☐6 ☐7 ☐8 ☐9 ☐10
_____
_____

"Is having a culture of service vital to our mission, values, and organizational identity?"

☐1 ☐2 ☐3 ☐4 ☐5 ☐6 ☐7 ☐8 ☐9 ☐10
_____
_____

"How do we measure our ability to do the important things?"

☐1 ☐2 ☐3 ☐4 ☐5 ☐6 ☐7 ☐8 ☐9 ☐10
_____
_____

"How important is it for us to create and develop OUR leaders?"

☐1 ☐2 ☐3 ☐4 ☐5 ☐6 ☐7 ☐8 ☐9 ☐10
_____
_____

"How important is it for you as an employee to feel engaged?"

☐1 ☐2 ☐3 ☐4 ☐5 ☐6 ☐7 ☐8 ☐9 ☐10
_____
_____

Chapter 2: Orientation Continues

What kind of test is this? I wondered. As I read the rest of the questions, I got the impression it was designed to see where we stood on issues of quality and organizational excellence. *Was he trying to identify if we had what it took to be officers in the department?*

It didn't take me long to score the questions with ones through tens. However, as I sat there, I just couldn't think of anything to write about each one. I looked around to see how the others were doing. I could tell most were like me—stuck. I was tempted to take the easy route and just put down my pencil. The tests didn't require our names, so no one would know.

What was the point of the test? I asked myself. *Obviously, they are looking for something.* With that I began to write.

After about 10 minutes, the chief came in again and looked around. "Looks like all of you are done with the test. Please pass them to the center and take out your blue folder. While you're doing that, let me introduce the next speaker, Chief Elle Black, division chief for EMS. She will tell you about a very important component of our jobs and the needs of the community."

The Blue and Green Folders

Thanks to showing up early this morning, I had already met Chief Black. I really hoped I had made a good impression on her. As she looked from one end of the table to the other, a PowerPoint presentation came up on the screen behind her. She began by telling us about the importance of EMS, and that this was the greatest opportunity to impact our customers. It sounded funny put that way. However, when 80 to 90 percent of the calls for service are EMS, I guess it made a lot of sense.

Chief Black went on to explain how EMS worked, what the paramedics and EMTs were doing when they were not in the firehouses, and more. She easily filled the hour without making it feel rushed. It didn't even look like Chief Black used a clicker to advance the pictures. She knew her material and how to get through it quickly.

As Chief Black finished, the fire chief came back and introduced us to Chief Goldbach. The head of training, he was the eldest of the chiefs. He was in his early sixties, and with a head of thinning gray hair and a handlebar mustache, he looked the part. Rumor had it that he had seen his fair share of fire but had been forced to transfer to administration because of an injury. He was well respected.

Everyone who presented to us today was a chief, which sure made it easy. No question as to who was in charge of what. I wondered if there were little political kingdoms in the department like those that often formed in regular offices. Being out in the firehouses, we didn't really get a feel for what went on in the administrative side of things.

Chief Goldbach's voice broke into my thoughts. "If you'll take out your green folder, let's take a look at what training is all about," he said. "Some of you may think it's all about preparation for the 'big one.' And in a way, it is. But it's also much more than that. Training is about keeping you safe no matter the circumstances.

"Let me give you an example," he continued. "At a fire, you can control only yourself and have influence over your crew. The building will not obey your commands to stay upright, nor will fire obey when you 'will' it to go out. Training is how we help you learn to control some variables and influence others in order to get the outcome you desire, even when there are so many factors working against you. At the fire scene, knowledge of fire behavior allows you to understand what may happen and take steps to mitigate the situation. Having learned the sounds a building gives when it is unstable alerts you to structural integrity. So, in short, training is developing not only your thinking processes, but your senses as well."

Boy, was he passionate! No wonder people liked to attend his classes and updates. He, like Chief Black, knew his job inside and out, and knew how to get us excited about what we were about to undertake. Some of the concern I had coming into the office this morning was gone. In fact, I could hardly wait to get back to the firehouse and practice some of what I had learned.

Chapter 2: Orientation Continues

We went through the green folder quickly. There was a lot in it, but Chief Goldbach assured us that most of it was research we would find handy later. Within the hour, he was finished. His presentation had turned out to be a whirlwind of valuable information.

And then, as if he had been cued by a light outside the door, the fire chief entered the room. "Thank you, Chief Goldbach. If I haven't mentioned it before, each of your presenters is available to you should you feel you'd like to bounce ideas, share concerns, or even get a little extra help. Remember, that's what we're here for—we're here for you. Now if you will, set aside the red, blue, and green folders, and place the purple one in front of you."

The Journey Folder

"This folder is different from the rest. This one does not contain documentation on what we do, why we do it, or how we do it. This folder has only three pages. The first page simply represents the Five Pillars of Service: People, Service, Quality, Finance, and Growth. We will not be spending a lot of time today on the foundation of how this organization is managed. You will find on this journey of discovery, however, that our organization is supported by those five pillars.

"When you look at the second page, you will see the Nine Principles® we strive to attain daily. If we can achieve these principles each day, I believe we will be successful. But it takes all of us. This is not a pie-in-the-sky formula. It takes work. If something doesn't work, we change it until it does.

"And lastly, you'll notice the Healthcare Flywheel®. This flywheel is not just applicable to healthcare. While it has specific healthcare applications—and as you have seen, much of our business is healthcare—it ties together the pillars and the principles.

"Now, I know you've had a long day. I'm sure you have questions, concerns, and ideas, so this is all we're going to do today. I do, however, have a few more things for you before we adjourn. I reviewed your tests and found that you are indeed the people we wanted to promote. Congratulations again! Before you leave today, I would like you to make an appointment for tomorrow with your division chief. This meeting will focus on how you fit into the organization, and your division chief will answer any questions you may have. Each chief has cleared his or her schedule for tomorrow, too, so that you will have the opportunity to meet with your chief and take as much time as necessary.

"One last item. Remember your homework. You are to find out about the people listed on page two of your organizational chart. Some of you have been given the same individuals. This is not an exercise to get the right answer.

"On Monday the 10th, I expect you here at 3:00 p.m. in uniform. Formal invitations have been mailed to the board members and each of your families, inviting them to the swearing in and pinning ceremonies to be held that afternoon. See you then." And with that, the chief turned and walked out the door. I looked at the clock above the door, and saw that it read exactly 4:00 p.m.

I pulled out the schedule. The afternoon had flown by. I knew we were done early, but I thought I'd check to see what time we were supposed to be done. To my surprise, we were scheduled to finish at 4:00 p.m.

I picked up my materials and went to Chief Black's office. I was a paramedic, so I was to schedule an appointment with her. As I got to her door, I noticed an envelope taped to it. It had my name on the outside. I opened the envelope, took out a piece of paper, and read:

Chapter 2: Orientation Continues

> Lt. Benjamin,
>
> I had to leave early and I apologize for the inconvenience. Please ask Sandy, our Division Secretary, to schedule our meeting. She will call me and let me know what time works for you.
>
> Thanks,
> Chief Black

I went to the secretary's desk and asked if I could make an appointment. The secretary pleasantly offered several times from which to choose. I decided on the early morning slot when things would be quieter. It would be my best opportunity to really concentrate.

CHAPTER THREE

THE HEALTHCARE FLYWHEEL COMES TO LIFE

More Questions Than Answers

After I got home, my head was still filled with all that had occurred. While some of the material given to us was new, most of it simply reinforced department policy, etc. But I kept going back to the folders—red, blue, green, and purple. *Was there a significance to the colors? If so, what was it?*

I laid the folders out in front of me on the dining room table. By far, the red one had the most papers in it. However, most of the material related to department operations. This would be some dry reading. The green folder had research from Harvard, the National Fire Academy, the *Journal of Emergency Medical Services*, and Firefighter Close Calls. Probably some interesting stuff on keeping my crew safe. The blue folder contained our protocols and resource materials. In a way, it was no different from the red folder.

I put all three aside. The purple one with the three pages intrigued me. *Why only three pages, and why purple?* I thought to myself. I took the pages out of the folder and spread them out in front of me.

Looking at the page titled "Five Pillars of Service: People, Service, Quality, Finance, and Growth," I understood how pillars supported the roof of a building. Similarly, I could see how the pillars of service supported an organization. I set this page aside. Like the pillars, I viewed the Nine Principles as something managers and executives learn in business school. Yet, those Nine Principles can greatly influence what we are capable of. *I need to look at these and how they fit into my job*, I thought. I put this page aside as well.

I grabbed the one about the Healthcare Flywheel. Looking at the circle—Passion, Principles, Pillar Results—it all made sense. *Okay*, I thought, *I have passion for what I do, I understand the need for principles, and I can see how pillar results indicate our success. But what does it all really mean?* I wondered. *Why did the chief give us these three pages without going into some detail? What are we supposed to learn or gain from this?* I had more questions than answers. I knew then that I was tired. It had not been a normal day for me, and I could feel it.

I started writing questions on the flywheel page. I wanted to find out the answers and what they meant to me as a newly promoted officer. After about 15 minutes, I had written seven questions:

1. Why a circle?
2. Does it have any relationship to the circle of life?
3. Why isn't what's in the middle of the circle on the outside?
4. How long have you been doing it?
5. Do you get tired of doing it over and over again?
6. What do you want to accomplish?
7. How do you keep thinking of new things to do or say?

I put the folders and their contents aside. *Better get something to eat before it gets too late*, I told myself. With that, I fixed dinner, watched the news on television, and relaxed. The rest of it would have to wait until tomorrow.

Chapter 3: The Healthcare Flywheel Comes to Life

The Morning Meeting

I woke early. Restless night. I just couldn't get the Healthcare Flywheel out of my mind. I showered, dressed, and headed to the administration building for my next meeting with Chief Black. *Today*, I told myself, *I will listen more and talk less.* It was a beautiful day and, as I drove to the building, I was looking forward to my questions about the flywheel being answered.

Once more, I arrived at the building around 6:30. Again, only one car in the parking lot—Chief Black's. However, I waited in my car. *Should I go in? Would it be too early? She obviously likes her quiet time. Will this disrupt her routine?* I sat in the car as long as I could, trying to be distracted by the music on the radio. It didn't work. *Better go in*, I thought.

I tried the front door again. You would think I would've learned the first time it was locked this early. *Too much on my mind, but at least I didn't almost walk into an unopened door again.* I headed for yesterday's entrance point.

Just as I came around the side, Chief Black was leaving the building. "Oh, good morning," she said.

"Morning," I said. "I hope you're not leaving on my account?"

She chuckled, "No, I forgot to bring in some important materials I worked on last night. Go on in. There's coffee!" With that, she headed for her car, unlocked it, and took out a bulky, expanding file folder.

But I waited, holding the door open for her re-entry. "I hope all of that's not for me today," I said.

She answered, "In some ways, yes—and in others, no. The chief has asked us to work on developing a service improvement program. This is just some of the research I have been doing."

We walked down the hall to the break room. Chief Black put her folder down at the table where I had found her yesterday. "Like to have a seat?"

I nodded and walked over to the table.

"So, what do you think?" she asked.

My mind flashed, *What do I think? About what?* But "Think?" was the only thing to come out of my mouth.

"About the new orientation program? Do you think we should keep it or scrap it for the old 'Just give me the badge and radio' one?"

I guess I should have given some thought to what we would talk about this morning before I came in. I had questions to ask, and now Chief Black was the one asking the questions. My thoughts revolved around the flywheel, but of course she'd want to discuss more than just that.

"Oh, I thought it was great. Gave us a better idea of what's expected," I answered.

"Now, you're just being polite. We gave you some tools. But we didn't really tell you our division expectations—that's why our meeting today was scheduled. But that's okay. I'll take the compliment," Chief Black said, smiling.

I guess no matter what I say, I am stepping in it.

"I'm sorry," I said. "I got so caught up in the questions I wanted to ask, I forgot that it's not always about me."

"That's okay. Hope it was an interesting day. We tried some new ideas to see if this orientation could be improved. That way, when people are promoted, they'll be able to see both sides of the situation—not just admins and not just 'the guys.' It will take some time, but with your feedback and others, I'm sure we'll be able to create a program to help future officers hit the ground running."

This was more than I expected. They were trying to change the "nothing to worry about formality" into something that made a difference. *Why now?* I wondered. *The department has been around a long time. It has survived all these years without a training program for new officers.*

As if reading my mind, Chief Black spoke. "I thought this was something new officers wanted. It's why the fire chief tasked us to provide you with an overview of how the department works. It was meant to show you what is available and how we can help you. Did we misread what you wanted?"

Chapter 3: The Healthcare Flywheel Comes to Life

"No," I said quickly. I didn't want her to get the impression I didn't want it—I only wondered what had taken them so long to realize it was needed. "I learned a lot yesterday. Having the opportunity to meet the chiefs and other new officers was terrific."

"That's good to hear," she said.

"But I do have some questions about what was presented."

"Good, let me get another cup of coffee and we can jump right in. Okay?" she asked, getting up and going over to the coffee pot. "Oh, before you get started, let me ask...was this what you expected when you heard about the orientation?"

"Not anywhere close. Maggie was even saying she didn't want to come because she thought it was a waste of time. When Pete, Maggie, and I left last night, we were all overwhelmed at how much really is going on."

"Interesting. I guess administration is a foreign place to you compared to being on the streets every shift," she said as she returned to the table.

"Not so much foreign, but there seems to be a communication gap."

"That's one of the disconnects we are addressing right now. Glad to hear you've identified it." Chief Black sat down at the table, moved aside her reading materials, and took out a blank piece of paper.

"Disconnects?" I asked.

"Sure, disconnects. When you think something is working well, only to find out it's not, and you don't know why. We've found that what we're communicating is not getting through to everyone, and we want to know why. Is it administration? Simply being out in the field? Is it how we present things? Or is it because the communication just isn't getting through the layers of staff? I don't have the answer for you today, but we *are* working on it."

I decided that if I said anything right now it would come out wrong. Chief Black was going 100 miles a minute. So I sat there and nodded.

With her paper ready and pen in hand, Chief Black sat back and said, "So, you have questions. Let's see where this takes us."

I pulled out the folders. I arranged them so that the red one was on the bottom, then the green on top of the red. This left the blue on top.

"Great, the only questions you have concern the items in the blue folder?" she said.

"No, I just hadn't gotten to the purple one yet."

As I pulled out the purple one, she said, "Whew, talk about putting me on the spot."

I placed the purple one on top. I opened it and pulled out the three sheets, placing the Healthcare Flywheel on the top. Chief Black's eyes scanned the page while I put the folder down on the table. I wasn't sure if she could read what I had written on the page or not, so I began.

"We were told we could ask questions about anything today. When I got home last night, I looked at the folders and this last one started me thinking," I said.

"Fire away," she replied.

The Flywheel Explained

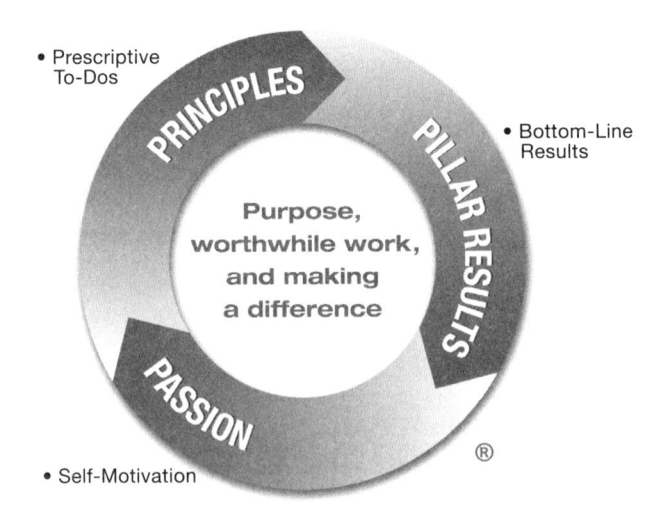

- Prescriptive To-Dos

PRINCIPLES

- Bottom-Line Results

PILLAR RESULTS

Purpose, worthwhile work, and making a difference

PASSION

- Self-Motivation

Chapter 3: The Healthcare Flywheel Comes to Life

So I began. "Why a circle for the flywheel? Does this have any relationship to the circle of life? Why isn't what's in the middle on the outside? How long have you been doing it? Do you get tired of doing it over and over again...?"

"Wait a minute," Chief Black cut in. "You're going way too fast. When you said you had questions, I thought you'd start with some easy ones, not jump right into the meat of the program," she said. "Let's start over. All right?"

"Okay. Why a circle for a flywheel? What's it mean?"

"That part is easy," she answered. "Without getting too technical, a flywheel is a rotating disk used as a storage device for kinetic energy. Remember what you learned in fifth grade? Kinetic energy is the energy an object possesses due to its motion. Once a flywheel starts moving, it resists changes to its rotation due to that energy. Only a force of the same magnitude returns the wheel to a state of rest. There's a whole mathematical formula dedicated to the kinetic energy of a flywheel, but we're not going to go into that here.

"Flywheels have been around for thousands of years in the form of a potter's wheel! The potter gets the wheel moving, and as he attempts to form the clay he applies resistance. Once the opposite forces he's applying have a greater effect and the wheel begins to lose momentum, the potter counteracts the resistance by giving a couple of short bursts to the wheel."

"I thought this was going to be an easy question," I said.

Chief Black chuckled. "It was, but I needed you to know how a flywheel works. Once it gets moving, it requires a little effort to keep it going, and a great effort to stop it. That's why we chose the flywheel—because each of us has the ability to keep the wheel turning, and it would take a greater effort to stop it once it's in motion. Now back to your question. Have you ever seen a square flywheel?"

This time I had to laugh. "I guess that was a pretty dumb question, wasn't it?"

Chief Black waved her hand in the air as if to bat away the statement. "By no means was that a dumb question. My explanation might have been a little long, but I think you understand the importance of the symbolism.

"Now let's transfer that symbolism to our organization. The flywheel represents how we need to operate if we are to go from being merely good to great. What puts the wheel *in motion* for us is at the very center of it: doing purposeful, worthwhile work. But what keeps it going?"

I stared at her. "Well, the satisfaction we get from what we achieve."

"Which is?"

"Saving lives, putting out fires, rescuing people from great danger…You know."

"Precisely," she agreed. "We make a difference, one that's easy to identify. In that respect, we're way ahead of other organizations where employees cannot see how they make a difference. So each of us has the ability to keep the wheel turning. What creates resistance?"

"Uh…burnout?"

"That's one thing. Think of it in different terms, though. Remember what I said earlier? As an organization, we're good…we save lives and do all the things we should to gain the community's respect. But how about being *very* good? That would require some changes, wouldn't it? And aren't people resistant to change? When the potter encounters resistance in his wheel, he gives it another burst of power. It will be up to the officers of our organization—such as you—to help the flywheel keep turning when there is resistance to the changes we want to put in place. Attitude plays a big part in this whole process."

My expression must have changed a hundred times while Chief Black was talking. There was a lot more to the symbolism of the flywheel than I had picked up on. "So I guess this has nothing to do with the circle of life?" I asked sheepishly.

"If you're thinking of the song from the Disney movie—not exactly. The circle of life operates on the belief in the interdependence and interconnection of all life. Human, animal, plant, and on and on. With the flywheel, there's an interdependence between what we do, how we do it, and the outcomes that impact human beings. When people feel

Chapter 3: The Healthcare Flywheel Comes to Life

connected, there is more energy. When they feel left out and put down, there is less energy. So I guess, in a way it does have something to do with the circle of life."

I asked the next question, "Why isn't what's in the middle of the circle on the outside?"

Chief Black looked at me and smiled. "How do you know when you're doing worthwhile work and making a difference?"

I just sat there and looked at her.

"Because we have certain feelings about the work we're doing. I can't name them, but I can tell you when I have them," I finally replied.

"Exactly! When the flywheel is in motion, spinning correctly, people feel they have a purpose or have performed worthwhile work. When people feel connected, there is more energy, and great things get accomplished. If those outcomes were on the outside of the wheel, they would spin off line, like putting a coin on a turntable. But when they are held in by the three parts of the flywheel, the wheel spins in constant motion, not losing momentum for the things we care about—the purpose, worthwhile work, and making a difference."

So far I had learned about physics, human nature, and mechanical engineering. I decided to hold my last two questions. Instead I asked, "So where did the flywheel concept come from?"

Creating a Great Place to Work

Chief Black looked at her watch and began. "A couple of years ago, the fire chief and I went to a conference on healthcare. We wanted to find out where healthcare was going in the future and how we fit into the picture. One of the speakers at the conference was Quint Studer of Studer Group® in Pensacola, Florida. He showed us the concept of the flywheel. He told us that the flywheel presentation was used to help us understand that creating great places to work was a journey. While the conference was about healthcare and helping physicians learn how to provide the highest quality care, the fire chief and I took away the idea that the flywheel was just as important for us.

"If it can work for nurses, doctors, and housekeeping staff, why not paramedics, EMTs, and first responders? If anything, pre-hospital care providers need the flywheel as much or more. Once the patient has been turned over to the doctors and nursing staff of the Emergency Department, there is little feedback received by these first responders except in quality control reviews.

"So the fire chief bought Mr. Studer's book *Hardwiring Excellence*. After he read it, he gave it to me. We decided to use the Healthcare Flywheel to assist us in creating the kind of organization we want to be a part of. The chief went out and bought each of the division chiefs their own copy so they could be on board with this as well.

"After that, the rest is history. We began to have meetings, brainstorming sessions, lunch 'n learns. We kept it close to home at first so that we could work out some of the details in dealing with the negative forces. Then we slowly started putting the principles in the book to work here. All that changed how we look at our employees, peers, and ourselves.

"The most obvious change is in the new officer orientation you're going through right now. Our goal is to teach you a new way of thinking. In giving you tools and listening to your needs, we discovered we already have the greatest employees."

This was more than I had expected. I thought I'd get some simple answers to my questions. But there was more to it, much more. I was beginning to wonder how much time the chiefs would be able to spend with us, or if this was just some noble experiment. Chief Black looked down at the table and then back up at me. "I know this is a lot to take in. If you like, I can loan you my copy of *Hardwiring Excellence*," she said.

"I'm a little overwhelmed right now. Could I take a rain check? There's a lot to think about, and I'm still trying to find my place as a new officer."

Chapter 3: The Healthcare Flywheel Comes to Life

"Sure, the offer stands. On another point, I know this is your day off, and I have a desk full of things to get accomplished. So could we continue this another time?" she asked.

My head was swimming from all the details she had given me. What a nice chance to slow down and take a breath. "That would be great," I told her.

"Terrific. Let's look for some time later in the week or on Monday when you come back in."

"Thanks, I appreciate that," I said, knowing full well I had a lot of catching up to do.

Back on Duty

The next day was my normal shift. I reported for duty at 7:00 a.m. Once I let the person I was to relieve know I was there, I went down to the truck bay to check out the fire engine. I took out the EMS bag to see if everything was ready for my shift. This was part of our normal routine. Check in, check the bag, check out what's for breakfast.

As I was closing the bag and about ready to put it on the truck, the engine lieutenant came up to me and asked, "So how was orientation? Get your badge and radio?"

I stood up, and he noticed that I wasn't wearing any bugles. Bugles are our identity. A person can see at a glance by the number of bugles on a collar what rank we hold and the honors we have attained.

"Whatsa matter? Get demoted already?" he asked in a lighthearted tone.

"No, we don't get pinned 'til next Monday. All we've done so far is go to the orientation session where each of the department chiefs spoke."

"Surprised you were able to wake up this morning, as boring as it must have been."

I smiled, not wanting the engine lieutenant to know I thought it was interesting. I just wanted to stay under the radar. This crew had a

35

tendency to play tricks on "newbies," sort of a ritual here. Get promoted—get practical jokes played on you.

"Well, good to see you survived. Nothing new to report. Looks like another day in paradise."

As the lieutenant walked away, I began to wonder, *Nothing new to report? What about Joe, the guy on "A" shift? I heard he had his knee operated on and would be out six months or more. How was he doing? I would go nuts if I had to lie around the house for six months because of an injury.*

Could this be what Chief Black was alluding to at our meeting? I guess this is part of the disconnect—no information about Joe or his condition. I'd have to remember to make a point of calling him today when I got a chance.

I placed the bag back in the compartment on the fire truck and closed the door. Just then, the engineer came up. His name was Tim, but we all called him Hoss.

"Where's your bugle? Fire you already? Or did they make you chief?" He laughed loudly. "You joining us for breakfast?"

"Yeah, I'll be right up," I replied. Hoss was one of the guys. He took care of those on his engine. If you needed something, he got it. I think he'd give you his uniform if you'd forgotten yours.

It took me a few minutes to make sure all the equipment was placed on the truck, including my protective gear. When I finally got upstairs, I could hear laughter as I walked down the hallway. When I rounded the corner and could see the table, everyone stopped laughing and became silent, shoveling food into their mouths.

"Looks great," I said as I sat down. The normal chatter at the table was definitely curtailed. *I wonder what happened*, I thought. I would have to talk to Hoss later to find out what was going on. Just then, the tones of an alarm went off, and everyone deserted the meal.

Once we arrived at the scene of an auto accident, things went like clockwork. People knew each other and could predict how each would respond. The patient was in good hands with this crew. As happens occasionally, the engine paramedic had to go to the hospital with the patient. Since this was my job, I went with the ambulance. When we cleared the hospital 45 minutes later, I talked with the ambulance crew. They'd heard a rumor that I was to be an engine company lieutenant, taking over my lieutenant's position. Now I had an idea about why the crew had gotten so quiet. When we returned to the firehouse, I knocked on the lieutenant's door.

"LT, got a minute?" I asked.

"Is this about your promotion?" he said.

"I'm not sure. But I need to ask you some questions. I don't know who to talk to today. Nobody seems to be saying much when I'm around," I replied.

The Bombshell

"Come on in and close the door."

I did as he requested. Then the lieutenant dropped the bombshell.

"Frank, you're no longer one of the guys. You're an officer now. They heard a rumor you pushed me out of my slot here in the firehouse and are taking over for me. I had planned on making the announcement at lunch because breakfast is usually pretty rushed getting equipment checks and the day plan out of the way."

"Planned on telling them what?" I asked.

"That you will be filling in for me for a few weeks. You're not pushing me out. I'm going to do something I've put off way too long. I'll be gone about 10 shifts."

"Ten shifts? That's a whole month. What am I going to do if I need help?"

"You'll be fine, but you need to learn your second lesson as a new LT. The rumor mill here flies like crazy. You know… you've been there. At the orientation you attended, did they talk about communication?"

I nodded.

"Good, well now we have some miscommunication, because I thought it best to announce my plans at lunch. Guess it worked out well anyway."

I wasn't in exact agreement with his statement, but I sure felt better.

The lieutenant continued, "Now we can show them how jumping to conclusions can hurt someone, and that if you have a question, don't be afraid to ask. Just like you did one-on-one with me. Guess you did learn something in that class. Before, I remember you jumping in with both feet before you had all the facts. Welcome to leadership. Let's go let them in on the real situation."

The lieutenant and I went out to the day room. Hoss was filling out the run report, and the rest of the crew was cleaning up from breakfast.

"Hey guys," the lieutenant called out. "How about a quick meeting?"

Everyone came into the day room, some still drying their hands from the dishes. "I want to put to rest the rumor that Frank is pushing me out the door."

They all looked at each other.

"As a matter of fact, I am taking some time off. I have almost 70 shifts of leave on the books, and I plan on retiring in about five years. Well, you know the policy: Use it or lose it."

Everyone laughed. It was not like the lieutenant to take any time off. We were his extended family. Fixing his fences, repairing his car. He was as much a part of our family as you could get.

The lieutenant went on to explain that he had requested I be assigned here instead of a more senior lieutenant coming into *his* house. He told us that since we all knew each other, it would make my transition to lieutenant smoother. Then he told everyone to watch out for me, which I didn't understand.

Later, he explained why when he told me my job responsibilities and what to expect. The reason he wanted his crew to watch out for me was because this firehouse was one of the most desired in the department. We got calls—good calls. Opportunities to make a difference.

Chapter 3: The Healthcare Flywheel Comes to Life

The lieutenant explained that if I wasn't available to take his place, another lieutenant might decide to bump him from his spot.

"Why is that?" I asked.

"We are the prize that people want to take over more and more. People are so blinded by ambition at times that you have to protect what's yours. In this case, our team. If another officer got a foothold in this firehouse, the team could be broken up and sent to different parts of the city. If my crew is watching your back, and you are watching theirs, it won't happen. And in 10 shifts, I'll be back. Do you understand?"

"Sort of," I said, nodding.

"Just watch out for each other, and remember, you have to earn their respect," the lieutenant continued.

We talked for a while longer. There was more to this officer stuff than I had expected. I envisioned being a good paramedic, giving orders, and having them followed, but now there was more to it. *I wonder how the Healthcare Flywheel fits into the picture?*

The rest of the shift was quiet. However, the phone kept ringing off the hook with people asking the lieutenant what was going on. Each time, he told the person on the other end that he was just taking some time off. I began to worry. It wasn't like him not to tell everyone what was going on. I remembered that when he and his wife went to Canada to do some skiing, we all knew where he was going and how long he would be gone. Not this time. I made a mental note to call him after he was off shift for a while rather than waiting to make my first call when I needed bailing out.

CHAPTER FOUR

WHAT MAKES THE FLYWHEEL TURN

Values and Passion

The next morning I decided to see if I could make another appointment with Chief Black. I called her office at about nine in the morning. Her secretary answered and told me I could see the chief that afternoon.

I showed up at the chosen hour, but Chief Black wasn't back yet from a previous appointment. Fifteen minutes later, she showed up a little out of breath. "Sorry, it was a meeting I couldn't miss. Can I get you something? Coffee, water?" she asked.

A moment later she returned, looking more composed, with a cold bottle of water for me and another cup of coffee for herself. "Better watch out; you know what they say about too much caffeine," I commented.

"Yeah, yeah," she waved it off, smiling. "So what can I do for you today?"

"I worked in the firehouse since we last met, and I got to experience not being 'one of the guys' anymore, and how important communication is with your crew. I just didn't think things traveled so fast in this department. I've always experienced a *lack* of information and communication, but now it seems I can't keep up!"

"Welcome to the big leagues," she said. "I'm glad you've had a chance to see a little of the problem. Not that our employees aren't the best in the world. They are! But sometimes organizational culture gets in the way. It's one of the barriers to great organizations. I think you'll find we have a few issues to work through, though I believe this organization is a good one."

I nodded and shrugged. "But mainly I'm here because I want to know more about the Healthcare Flywheel.®"

"Let's see…" Chief Black paused, collecting her thoughts. "When we last spoke, we talked about Purpose, Worthwhile Work, and Making a Difference, which are the hub of our Healthcare Flywheel. These are our values, which help center our organization and ourselves. Values keep the flywheel balanced and everything else from spinning off. They're what keep the momentum going. And we talked about the three things that make up our Healthcare Flywheel; namely, Passion, Principles, and Pillar Results," she said.

"That's true, but how does the flywheel get started?" I asked.

"Let's go back to values—the core of our flywheel. Who do you know who believes our values come first and foremost?"

"We all do, every day, in every firehouse," I answered.

"So then, what you are saying is that this organization already has what it takes to go from good to great?"

"Of course. Then why do some give everything they have and others only a little?"

"Take out your Healthcare Flywheel. Look at it. Study it. What do you see?"

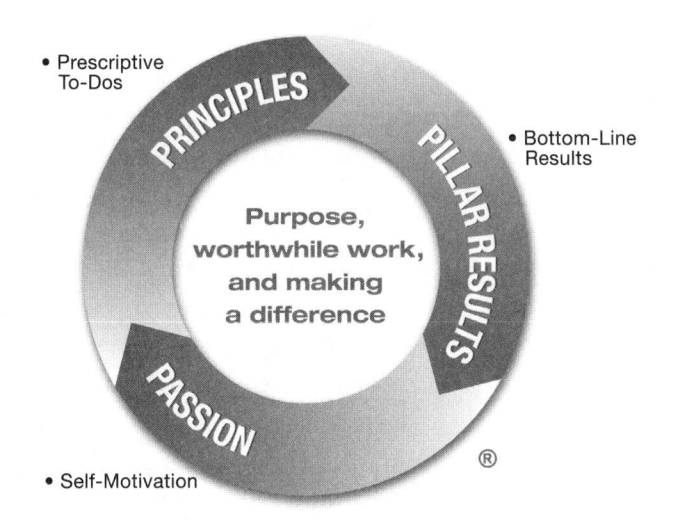

Chapter 4: What Makes the Flywheel Turn

- Prescriptive To-Dos
- **PRINCIPLES**
- **PILLAR RESULTS**
- Bottom-Line Results
- Purpose, worthwhile work, and making a difference
- **PASSION**
- Self-Motivation

"A circle that has no beginning or end. It goes around and around and around," I answered.

"And we have our values in the middle, which everything else revolves around. Look closer…do you see problems or potential?" Chief Black asked.

"Both," I responded.

"See, now you're getting it. With problems come opportunities to provide service. If we didn't have fires, we wouldn't have fire departments. If people didn't get sick, we wouldn't have hospitals. Overly simplistic, but it proves the point. So we have our values in the middle, which everything revolves around. Correct?"

I nodded.

"What gets the flywheel going is passion. But first you have to have burning commitment to those values before you can be passionate about the work you do. When you entered this field, you were already committed to certain behaviors, such as helping people, providing the best medicine possible, and taking care of your fellow man. If you and others like you had no commitment, the flywheel would wobble. You had that passion from the very first day."

I was beginning to feel like someone without much exposure to management, which was not true. However, I should have seen the things she was talking about.

"You also had the passion to go on and be a paramedic. Why? You could have simply gone along with the notion that first responder was good enough. Right?"

"Yes, but I thought if I continually improved my skills, I could do more for the people I served," I answered. "That would make it possible for me to enjoy what I do and help more people along the way."

"Great. Passion is more than wanting to do something. Passion is being self-motivated, or as Webster said, 'Passion is the emotion of feeling strongly about something.' It's also challenging yourself when you don't have to. That is self-motivation. Do you see how these go hand in hand?"

"Yes, I do!"

"So let's take it to the next level. Who but a self-motivated person would try everything he could for a dying patient, knowing his actions may not be successful? Or hold a dying infant in his arms to get care when others stood by and watched? Who but a self-motivated person could help someone else by establishing an intravenous line while in a ditch during the middle of the night with sleet falling around him? Shivering and cold, trying to infuse warm fluids into the patient. Or enter a burning building, and run to danger when others are running away? Who but a self-motivated person could do that, day after day, and still come to work for more of the same?

"It is no different for nurses or doctors," Chief Black continued. "They're faced with the same pressures, consequences, and outcomes, although they generally don't operate in the cold or in a hostile environment. The Healthcare Flywheel is a tool to identify our strengths, weaknesses, and means to take our organization to the next level. But without passion and self-motivation, the wheel would never even begin to turn.

"The problem we're experiencing today is that we unintentionally *de-motivate* our best and brightest. We deplete their passion instead of feeding it. This is especially true in the fire and emergency services.

"Remember the television show *Emergency!* in the 1970s? James Page was a battalion chief for Los Angeles County Fire Department. Well, he broke the mold for fire service EMS. In a way, he broke the mold for how *all* EMS is performed. Everyone now expects, not hopes for, highly skilled first responders to answer the call. Patients assume EMS people can talk to doctors and nurses from the field and get the necessary lifesaving orders. They *expect* that with a simple phone call, they can get the quality care they deserve.

"Today, this means we need to keep current on an ever-growing number of medications and procedures. New and challenging technology is released daily to help us do our jobs more effectively.

"These are all factors that can overwhelm and de-motivate not only first responders, but EMTs and paramedics as well. And they're issues faced throughout the entire healthcare industry.

"*Emergency!* did great things to get EMS started. If you look at what they had to work with in those days, it was the dark ages when compared to the advanced lifesaving techniques and equipment we have today. You are a part of that history—something to be proud of. But we're not done. We have to take it to the next level.

James O. Page
Photo courtesy of the County of Los Angeles Fire Department

"I can recommend a good book if you'd like to know more about how EMS got started. It includes how an underserved group in Pittsburgh created the first modern paramedic ambulance service. Have you ever heard of them?" Chief Black asked.

I didn't remember Pittsburgh as the beginning of EMS. I had always attributed that to Los Angeles. "No, I haven't."

"Well then, I think you may have some reading to do. The book is called *The Paramedics—An Illustrated History of Paramedics in their First Decade in the USA* by James Page. Why don't you read it when you have time or are having a low moment? This book will help inspire you to be the best paramedic you can be."

I wrote the name down, although I wondered when I'd have time to fit this in along with my other duties.

"Sorry I went off on a tangent," the chief said. "Let's get back to the Healthcare Flywheel. You see, passion and self-motivation only get the flywheel started. It begins to turn based on our values and is pushed by our motivation. It keeps turning when its energy is fed.

"Here is something I would like you to do. Think about what motivates you and make a written list. On the page, draw a line down the middle. On the left side at the top, write 'motivates,' and on the other side, write 'zaps my energy.' Make a list of those things that fit into one side or the other. Write them down at the moment you think of them. Don't wait until later. Do this for one day. At the end of the day, take out your list and see which things you really control. Do you control your motivation? Or do you control your de-motivation?

"Once you've done that, let's get together again. We'll talk about what you discovered and continue with the Healthcare Flywheel. Okay?"

I was feeling like this meeting was ending too quickly. And Chief Black had given me more to think about. But why? Where was all of this going?

"Sounds like a good idea," I said. "I have a lot to think about. Do you think we'll be finished by the time we have the swearing in ceremony?"

"There's a lot to the flywheel. I wouldn't push so hard to finish before the ceremony. Let's play it by ear."

"Thanks, I appreciate your time." With that, I got up to leave.

Chief Black said, "Good luck. You have entered into a brand new world. I hope I am helping."

"Thanks again," I said as I reached the door. *I didn't realize asking a few questions would mean so much more work*, I thought to myself as I left.

Chief Black Makes Her Rounds

Before I left, I went down the hall in search of the finance department to ask a question. Ten minutes later, I was headed for the exit door when I saw Chief Black again. Holding a clipboard, she was talking in earnest to a couple of admin employees.

I heard her say, "Is there anyone I should be rewarding and recognizing today for going above and beyond?"

One of them mentioned the name of a paramedic, telling her a story about how that person stopped by the hospital to visit someone he'd treated for smoke inhalation at the scene. The patient couldn't stop talking about it afterwards, and it eventually got back to the ambulance crew, who relayed it to the admin employee.

The chief smiled, writing on her clipboard as fast as she could. Next she asked, "Do you have the tools and equipment to do your job?"

They answered in the affirmative. Then, "Do you know of anything we could do better?"

The two looked at each other and shrugged. "Not really."

"Okay," Chief Black said. "Thanks for your time. You know where to find me."

I watched as she moved on to another area, where I could hear her repeat the litany of questions, starting with, "What is going well today?"

Curious, I walked up to the desk of one of the employees she had just questioned. I introduced myself, shook his hand, and said, "I've just been promoted to lieutenant, so I'm pretty new and this is only the second time I've been in admin. Tell me, does the chief often grill you like that?"

He grinned. "Man, that's not grilling. That's just the chief. She does that nearly every day, picks out a few of us to talk to, always has the same questions. She calls it 'rounding.'"

That stopped me in my tracks. I'd never heard of a senior officer doing this. "Is it something new?"

"Yeah, kind of. Been going on a few months now."

"What's the purpose of it?"

"Chief Black does it mainly to keep on top of things. If there's something we need, you better believe it's here before you can blink an eye. And she loves to hear about people doing extra things, you know, beyond what the job calls for. She'll tell everyone she meets now about that paramedic who visited the patient. And you know what else? She will send a thank-you note to that guy's home thanking him for doing it.

"Last time she was through here, John over there," he pointed to another employee, "told her we needed to improve how we communicate. He suggested everyone get together at the start of the day for a 10-minute briefing. She was so excited you'd have thought she won the lottery! And you know what else? A memo just came down telling us that effective next month, we'll be having what she calls a 'daily huddle' at the start of the day to keep each other up to speed on what we're working on.

"Bottom line, she listens to us and acts on it. Couldn't ask for a better chief."

I thanked him and headed for the door.

Chapter 4: What Makes the Flywheel Turn

Letting It Sink In

My head was still spinning when I got home. *What have I gotten myself into?* I thought. The house was quiet. Even the dogs didn't come greet me when I walked through the door. *Where were the dogs?*

I realized how beat I was. Too much information—TMI! How was I going to be able to do my job, balance the promotion orientation, and be a good husband? I could hardly wait for my wife to return from her trip so I would have someone to bounce ideas off of. I dragged myself into the kitchen and opened the refrigerator. Nothing good. I guess I wasn't really that hungry. You could bet even money, however, that the dogs were. I had left the dogs in the sunroom so that the house would be clean for my wife's return. Well, it really wasn't a sunroom at all, just painted yellow and bright with doors to the outside.

There were three sets of eyes staring at me. Their tongues were hanging out the sides of their mouths, and their tails were wagging ferociously. Sometimes I thought those tails should be registered as lethal weapons.

"Okay, okay, settle down," I told my waiting audience. "Did you miss me?" I petted each dog in turn and retrieved their dishes. Walking to the garage where we kept the dog food, I lapsed back into my earlier thoughts. *Was I making this more than it really was? Was I taking this all too seriously?*

I heard a bark, which snapped me back to reality. "Well, I guess I had better take care of you first, or I'll never be able to concentrate," I said to no one in particular. I scooped up the dogs' food and returned to find them sitting patiently. They gave me "the look." Six eyes staring at the bowls of food, drool in a puddle on the floor, and an occasional half-jump to let me know that they knew I had FOOD. It was our normal ritual. These guys thrived on ritual.

Yuck, I thought. *I hope it tastes better than it smells.* I went back into the kitchen and dug through the refrigerator for my dinner. I finally settled on a Tupperware dish with leftovers from the day before. *Better get rid of this before Lexi gets home.* I opened the lid and placed

49

the dish in the microwave. In a few short seconds, my meal would be cooked, hot, and ready to eat. I set the time on the microwave and went to get the notes I had taken earlier in Chief Black's office.

I stared at the notes, not really reading them, just gazing at the papers. *Am I ready to tackle this right now?* With that thought, the buzzer on the microwave beeped. *I think I'll eat first and think second.*

After I finished my dinner, I took the dishes and put them in the dishwasher. *Maybe I should play with the dogs for a few minutes so I won't feel guilty for spending so much time at the office.*

I went into the garage and found three different toys. Dogs, like children, all seem to have different personalities. The big dog likes his Frisbee, the oldest a stuffed bear, and the youngest a tennis ball. With toys in hand, I wandered out to the backyard so that I could throw for one and tug with another while the third was retrieving the previously thrown toy. *If I can balance this, surely I can balance a simple promotion!*

After about 15 minutes, the dogs began to tire. "Okay guys, time to go inside and get some water."

The dogs quickly jumped through the special door we had installed just for them. *One of the best investments I ever made*, I chuckled to myself. *It sure makes life easier.*

I went back to my notes on the table. *Take a piece of paper, draw a line down the middle, label one side "motivators" and the other side "energy zappers."* I got a blank sheet of paper and did exactly that. I stared at the paper for a few moments and decided to work on it in the sunroom. I could accomplish two tasks at once: working on my paper and making the dogs feel like they were getting attention. I guess I was stalling, but I was wiped out.

After jotting down some "motivators" and "energy zappers" and playing with the dogs, I looked up at the clock. In a brief amount of time, I had listed 10 or 15 items under each category. I decided to see if I could set some appointments for the interviews I needed to conduct. As luck would have it, I was able to schedule each of them on my next duty day. All of the people I was assigned not only agreed to the interviews, but set the times and places as well.

Chapter 4: What Makes the Flywheel Turn

To make things even better, the first person on my interview list, the battalion chief, had checked the duty roster and noted that no one was assigned as the battalion aide for the day—so he appointed me! This assignment was normally delegated to senior-level personnel, but the chief was willing to work with me so I could complete the interview and get another perspective on the department.

I thought about Chief Black's "rounding" procedure. I would have to find out where it fit in with keeping the flywheel turning. *It was something I could do for my people.*

Time for bed—tomorrow my wife would be home!

TACTICAL CONSIDERATIONS

Throughout this book we'll talk about the basics of how we make the flywheel continue to turn. It doesn't happen by magic. There are tactics to accomplishing the principles behind the flywheel. Tactics simply mean "a system or mode of procedure." So, tactical considerations in our case mean a system by which we work to create a GREAT organization. In this chapter, Chief Black demonstrated one of the tactics:

Focus on Employee Satisfaction

In healthcare, one way leaders communicate with employees while simultaneously focusing on satisfaction is the tactic known as "Rounding for Outcomes." You could simply call it "Engaging Your Employees." You do this by getting out of your office to observe and talk with the team. As you are out and about, ask:

1. What is working well today?
2. Are there people I should be recognizing today for outstanding effort?

3. Is there anything we can do better?
4. Do you have the tools and equipment to do your job?

When you're done, make sure you follow up on what you learned. If you hear that Captain John Smith did an outstanding job on this or that call, send him a note letting him know you appreciate the effort he extended. He'll not only feel better about the job he's done, he'll want to repeat the behavior and will be motivated to continue working hard for the organization. You can really make the flywheel hum if you send the note to Captain Smith's home where he'll share it with his family. Plus, if you include the name of the person who told you in the first place about the captain, this will also relate favorably in the working relationship between Captain Smith and the person who mentioned him.

Surveys tell us that, no matter the industry, employees want three things:

1. They want to believe *the organization has the right purpose*.
2. They want to know *that their job is worthwhile*.
3. They want to *make a difference*.

These same principles are what drive our flywheel. Emergency services could very easily focus on the negative. Remember, we're dealing with and responding to people's worst days. However, when you round and learn about opportunities to reward and recognize someone, you're focusing on the positive. This reminds employees that they do make a difference and that their jobs are worthwhile.

Likewise, if you learn that tools and equipment are not working properly, follow up and fix what you heard about. This tells the crew you care about them.

Focusing on employee satisfaction is not a quick fix. It is a process, and it takes time and work. You can't wait for the perfect time to start. Conditions will never be perfect. **You have to start and you have to act. Now.**

CHAPTER FIVE

PURPOSE, WORTHWHILE WORK, MAKING A DIFFERENCE

The Reunion

When I got to the airport, I learned that my wife Lexi's plane was delayed 45 minutes. With the new Homeland Security rules, I couldn't meet her at the gate, but had to wait outside the security area. I went to a gift shop, bought a magazine, and sat down to read. Before I knew it, a half-hour had passed, and I decided to go to the waiting area. As I arrived, my wife waved, smiled, and walked faster toward the exit.

Boy, was I glad to see her. When we finally got to hug, we shared how much we'd missed each other. After picking up Lexi's bags, we walked to the car with Lexi chattering all the while about her trip and the exciting possibilities it had opened up for her. It had been a long time since I had seen her so excited about anything.

When we got to the house, I could see that Lexi was exhausted and running on fumes. We had a quick dinner, and she went to unpack. About 15 minutes later, I went to see if she needed any help, only to find her sound asleep. I covered her with a blanket and went back into the living room. Thoughts of the upcoming promotion ceremony filled my head. Lexi would be there to pin on my badge, and that seemed to calm my mind. I decided it was time for sleep, too. We could talk tomorrow.

With that, I made my way to bed. I reached over to Lexi, kissed her gently on the forehead, and said, "Goodnight. I am so happy to have you home." She didn't make a sound. But she smiled and curled her body into mine.

The next morning I was up early. I don't know why, but my eyes opened at 4:30 a.m. I must have looked at the alarm clock at least five times.

Is it only 4:30? I thought to myself. I tried to close my eyes and go back to sleep, but it was no use. I got up, made coffee, and looked at my notes again. Today I felt different. I had a positive energy. It was like I could really feel it. I had a chance to make a difference.

Taking a chance, I fixed breakfast and carefully placed it on a tray along with a large cup of coffee. I walked into the bedroom to find Lexi stretching and whisking the sleep from her eyes.

"Good morning. Sleep well?"

"I must have been tired. When did I fall asleep?" she asked.

"Shortly after you got home."

"I must have slept really well. What time is it?"

"About 5:00," I responded.

"That early?" she said in surprise.

"Well, you have been gone awhile, and I'm sure the time change didn't help. Before I drop something, let me set down this tray so you can have breakfast in bed."

"Coffee. I need coffee."

I definitely knew this was not a request. I bent down to place the tray on Lexi's lap and handed her the coffee.

"Breakfast is served, my lady."

"Mmm, this is heaven," she mumbled sleepily.

"Enjoy your breakfast. I need to get ready for work," I said as I left the room. I had just enough time to shower, change, and get to the firehouse before shift change. I also needed to get my gear since I was to be the battalion chief's aide today.

Chapter 5: Purpose, Worthwhile Work, Making a Difference

Reporting for Duty

Traffic was lighter than I had expected, and I got to my firehouse in record time. I briefly exchanged hellos as I grabbed my equipment, returned to the car, and drove to the battalion chief's headquarters.

"Good, you're here early," the battalion chief said when he saw me. "Coffee?"

"No, thanks."

"I forgot to tell you that the battalion chiefs change shifts an hour before the other crews do. That way, we can be prepared if any issues should arise during shift change. Got your stuff, I see. We have you bedding down over here," he said as he led me down a hallway. "Not the Ritz, but all the chiefs' drivers bunk down here. Questions?"

I shook my head "no" in response.

"Good. Get comfortable, do what you need to do, and I'll see you in my office at seven o'clock." With that, the chief spun around and went back down the hallway towards the kitchen.

After settling in, I went downstairs to the chief's vehicle. It was a typical four-door SUV, painted with the department's color scheme and logos, light bar, and siren. Inside was a command center with radio, computer, small desk, fire extinguisher, clipboards, and more. I carefully placed my protective gear under the desk in the back to keep it out of the way.

While there, I checked out the passenger compartment and the driver's seat. I hadn't been told if I should drive or not. I didn't want to look stupid, so I checked to make sure both doors were unlocked—I would follow the chief's lead.

As I looked up, I saw the engineer from the fire engine coming down the stairs.

"Good morning," I said.

Looking a little startled to see me, he yawned and said, "Morning," as he got into "his" fire engine. He climbed in, started the engine, and climbed back down. I watched as he checked the gauges on the outside of the truck, worked some of the controls, and then climbed back in the cab. Just then the bay doors to the firehouse began to rise. When they were fully opened, the engineer pulled his truck around to the fuel pumps.

This morning routine was performed all across the city, and probably around the world. You make sure your equipment is ready for the next shift, leaving it in the same condition or better than when you got it. While truck checks are required, it's also a matter of pride among the firefighters and engineers to make that truck shine for the next crew. In most businesses, the supplies are first come, first served. You're constantly scrounging to find staples for the stapler, and it's man-eat-man when it comes to coffee or sodas. In our world, however, the men and women of the previous shift "provide you a service" by making sure that the fire engine is ready and in top shape for you when it is passed down.

It was the first time I realized that our people take care of "our people." I had always looked at the morning routine as something we just did. But now, I could see that this tied directly into the Healthcare Flywheel®. This "self-motivation"—the act of getting the equipment, ambulance, and even the chief's vehicle ready for the next shift—helped make the wheel turn.

I looked around the firehouse. The oncoming crew was arriving, joking, and talking with the on-duty crew. I glanced down at my watch. 6:58 a.m. I knew I'd better hurry and get to the chief's office.

Interview with the Battalion Chief

I took a deep breath as I arrived at the chief's office. I didn't feel that I was good at interviewing people. *I wish I had prepared for this interview*, I thought to myself. I didn't like being unprepared, and as a matter of fact, took pride in the fact that I thought ahead when dealing with situations on the emergency scene. *Why hadn't I thought to come up with some questions?*

Chapter 5: Purpose, Worthwhile Work, Making a Difference

I knocked on the door and heard a muffled, "Come in."

As I entered the battalion chief's office, I felt like I was transported back in time. The furnishings were nothing to brag about, but they were functional. There was a wooden desk that looked like it was about 60 years old, well kept and maintained, shiny, and not a scratch on it. Almost a museum piece. The battalion chief sat comfortably in an old leather chair that matched the desk.

On the walls were pictures of fires from around the city—the big ones—the ones that made the news. Some of the frames held the actual newspaper clippings. In between the pictures were items you would find in a firefighting buff's home: hose ropes, hydrant wrenches, fire brands, miscellaneous pieces, and an old Gamewell alarm. On top of the file cabinets and on shelves were brass nozzles, a small collection of toy fire trucks, family pictures, and more. The paneling behind all this stuff looked like it was original to the firehouse, built in the early 1900s, and it, too, was clean and well oiled.

There were oak bookcases filled with memorabilia as well as books on firefighting lore, firefighting tactics and strategy, the history of the fire service, prevention practices, emergency medical services, a binder with "SOPs" written on the spine—practically every square inch of space was taken. As I tried to take in this cornucopia, a voice broke through my wandering thoughts.

"Hi, Benjamin, grab a seat. I'll be with you in a minute."

I looked around to see where there could possibly be room for a chair. Near the corner of the chief's desk, I saw a chair. It was metal chrome with a fabric seat. Compared to the room's décor, it looked totally out of place.

I sat down and took out my notebook, quickly scribbling some questions I thought I might ask. After a couple of minutes, Chief O'Reilly spoke.

"So what's on your mind, kid?"

"Chief, as a part of the officer orientation, the fire chief gave us a list of individuals he wants us to interview, and you're first on my list."

"What does he want you to ask?"

"He didn't really say! He said we were to get to know you."

"You want to know about me?" the chief asked with a low rumbling laugh. "How much time you got, kid? Never mind. Let me tell you my story."

Chief O'Reilly told me that when he was young, growing up in New York City, he would race the fire trucks down the street until they arrived at what he called a "job." Kids always wanted to follow the fire trucks. "At times," he said, "if you weren't the fastest kid on the block, you didn't get to see nothin'. All the bigger kids would stand in front and you saw only their backs."

This was how he got the bug to be a fireman. He became the fastest runner in the neighborhood, and sometimes he was quick enough to see firefighters "ladder" the building. They would make heroic rescues, exiting with steam coming off their coats, black soot around their mouths and noses, and someone in their arms.

He went on to say that the fire service had changed a lot since he went into it so many years ago. "But it's still a fraternity where we take care of each other. You understand that?" he asked.

"I do."

The chief continued, reminiscing on how he advanced through the ranks and about the sacrifices he made to become a chief officer. He told how he learned to be a good officer by "reading" the smoke and the building. After about 20 minutes, he paused regaling his story and hung his head.

"What's wrong, Chief?"

"Just thinking about all the guys who didn't come back. It's tradition; it's a fraternity. We gotta care about our boys," he said.

I wrote down a few of his stories in my notes, but what stuck with me was his fierce belief in taking care of his team and his feeling that firefighting is more than just a job. He believed it was a calling.

Chapter 5: Purpose, Worthwhile Work, Making a Difference

Engine 15 Responds

Just then, the alarm tones broke into our conversation.

"Engine 15, Rescue 1, Truck 17, Battalion 3, respond to a collapse at the construction site—1505 University Blvd. Multiple casualties. Time out 7:35."

The station atmosphere switched instantly from "waiting" to "action." We became all business. "Get in the truck, kid; you're driving," Chief O'Reilly said to me. As we traveled the quickest route to the scene, he asked what I should be thinking about regarding the emergency, and in particular, how I would size up the situation, what my priorities were, and how best to assign units.

"Well, first I'd implement the ICS (Incident Command System) protocols and do an on-scene size-up. I can't make too many decisions until I see what we've got," I stated.

"Good answer, kid, but you need to be playing out some of these situations in your mind before ya get there," he said. "Ya gotta be thinking about your priorities from the start. What's your priority on this job?"

"Safety," I responded.

"Good, but whose?"

"Our people first, then the rescuers, then the victims..."

He cut me off. "Turn here, that way we can stay out of the way of the rigs."

Even while teaching me how to do a size-up, he was reminding me to let responders stage in closer to the scene.

"Ya don't get to see jobs like this very often!" he said, smiling like a kid who was playing with a new toy. Not missing a beat, he grabbed his mike, gave an on-scene size-up of the situation, placed his units, and began managing the incident.

It was then that I saw the magnitude of his passion. He was a doer. Not someone who was content to sit back and watch life pass him by. Thinking about what Chief Black had told me about the Healthcare Flywheel®, I could see Chief O'Reilly's purpose was to protect "his people," and that gave him value. It kept him on balance. Everything revolved around his desire to care for his team, which made his work worthwhile. His passion got the wheel to spin, but what held it in the center was his purpose—to take care of his team.

The scene was chaotic. People rushing here and there, calling for equipment, tools, trauma kits, and so on. Yet, through it all, the chief stayed calm as he watched his crew go through their paces, confident in their abilities to do their jobs.

The radio broke in. "Command, this is Rescue 1. We have a party trapped below a slab of concrete. We need additional resources at our location and a paramedic."

"Rescue 1, this is Command. Party trapped, need additional resources with heavy tools and medic."

"Message understood," came back the response from Rescue 1.

"Okay, kid, time to go to work. I need you as a medic now; you can learn later," the chief said. By the time I got all of my gear on, he was assigning additional units and calling for a "second alarm." I hurried off to assist the crews working on the collapse of a supporting beam at a new building under construction.

Things happened so fast. I was talking to my patient, establishing a "line," and the next thing I knew, the door was closing on the ambulance. The paramedic on the ambulance and I worked together maintaining the patient's airway and managing his bleeding. The fire crews did a great job of packaging the patient for transport, so we didn't have to do a lot of stabilization of possible fracture sites. This allowed one of us to communicate the patient's status while en route as the other medic delivered the best care possible.

Once at the hospital, the Emergency Department personnel took over. After we retrieved our backboard and replacement supplies, I called Chief O'Reilly. At that point, he was passing on vital information in a nearby firehouse as part of his duties. I arranged for the ambulance crew to take me there so I could meet up with him. As it happened, the captain of that firehouse was my next interview. I had missed my scheduled time by several hours, but I thought he would understand.

Chapter 5: Purpose, Worthwhile Work, Making a Difference

The Business Side of Firefighting

I got to the station just in time for lunch. I put my gear inside the bay doors and reported to Alastair Fletcher, one of the youngest captains in the department's history. He had joined the department fresh out of college where he had majored in engineering. He would have had a promising career with a major firm, but, as he tells it, he wasn't cut out to be a desk jockey.

A tall, sinewy man, Captain Fletcher didn't look anything like the seasoned battalion chief with whom I had just spent part of the morning. In his mid-thirties, the captain maintained an athletic physique and an attitude that encouraged others to do so as well.

"Captain, my name is Frank Benjamin. I had an interview scheduled with you today. I apologize for being late. Had to run a call and got here as soon as I could."

"Great to meet you. Store your stuff. Had lunch yet?" he asked.

I shook my head, as I hadn't had time.

"Hey, Grover, got enough for a wayward soul to sit down with us at lunch?" he yelled to the person at the kitchen counter.

"Sure, cap'n. Hope he likes gumbo. It'll be ready in about 15 minutes!"

"Fair enough. Go put your stuff next to the engine and wash up. I'll see you in about two minutes in my office."

I headed off to the locker room and made sure that I was quicker than the two minutes the captain had given me. I was already pushing the envelope by being late. Plus, I wanted to get as much information as I could from him.

I knocked on the door to his office.

"Come in, Frank, let's not stand on ceremony."

"Thanks, captain. You know about the interview, I hope?"

"Sure, the fire chief let us know he was assigning certain officers, new lieutenants, to us. His instructions were to tell you whatever you wanted to know about being an officer, working with the crews, and about us. Is that your understanding?"

Captain Fletcher had more information than I did. We were told only to "find out about each officer." I had already gotten information from Chief O'Reilly that was more in depth than just "finding out about him." It appeared that the fire chief had set us up to discover a lot in these interviews.

I simply nodded in response to Captain Fletcher's question.

"Good, so what do you want to know?" he asked.

Should I stick to the basics, like his background, how he got into his position, what he likes and dislikes? Okay, basics.

"What exactly is your job here?" I asked, and then immediately thought, *What a lame question. I hope he doesn't think I'm simply going through the motions.*

"Well, I thought you might have some tough questions for me, but you threw a soft one. Trying to get me warmed up first?" He didn't wait for an answer. "My job is like that of all managers, to be able to produce the best product for the most effective cost."

"Sounds to me like you're an entrepreneur or businessman, not a firefighter."

"In a way, I am. Let me explain. The customers we serve receive a product or service from us just as if we were a bank, dry cleaner, or any other for-profit business. Like the electric company, we provide our service 24/7. However, we're not like them in the fact that when the customer doesn't have any power or lights, the customer doesn't pay for a product. Therefore, the power company wants to get them back on line quickly so that they can purchase more power.

"Our service is a little different. People call us because they have a problem. Child locked in a bathroom, a fire, medical condition, cat in the tree, you name it. Yet, in each of these examples, there's a cost and a benefit. The cost of electricity is a bill paid monthly. The cost of our service is paid in taxes. The benefits are plain, I hope."

"Sure they are," I responded. "The benefit to electric customers is that their refrigerators continue to run, cooling their food, and the lights come on when the switch is flipped. The benefit we provide is a little peace of mind and security—they can sleep at night knowing that if they have an emergency, someone will be there to help. Right?"

Chapter 5: Purpose, Worthwhile Work, Making a Difference

"You've got the cost/benefit idea. The biggest difference is that the power company charges, and people pay for what they use. In our case, they pay even if they don't use the service. Here is where it gets messy—even if someone can't afford the service, we still provide it. Not like the power company, which turns off the meter if you don't pay. We still make the house calls regardless of a person's ability to pay."

I understood what he was saying. It made sense. Not too many people look at the Fire Department as a business, I thought.

"Now this would not be possible if somebody didn't work to make the service affordable. Money doesn't grow on trees. Therefore, government needs to provide that service as economically as possible. That's the fire chief's job. Yet, it's everyone's job. We look to see what we do, how we do it, and do what we can to prevent having to make the service calls. For instance, we provide fire prevention programs and health screenings. Fire prevention reduces the number of fires we respond to, and those we do encounter have better outcomes for our customers. Health screenings, as you have been doing, help us to identify potential health problems so the patient or customer can get treatment from a doctor outside the emergency environment. This makes it less costly for insurance companies and patients. Plus, we don't have to send emergency crews on a call at two o'clock in the morning, which costs the community in gas, maintenance, and equipment."

Boy, I thought to myself, *I didn't realize the Fire Department had such an economic impact on our community and how tied we are to a cost/benefit approach to service analysis. I hope he was joking when he said "warmed up."*

Meaningful Purpose

"That's just part of my job," Captain Fletcher continued. "It's the part you don't see. Another part of my job is to be a babysitter—no disrespect intended—counselor, confidante, manager, family member, coach, leader, and follower. I am sure you could attach a lot of titles to it. These are the roles I fill daily."

"I'll bet you could, captain. What motivates you to come to work, or is the greatest part of your job?" I asked.

"That's easy! The work I and the others on this crew do is worthwhile. We make a difference in people's lives. People trust us to do the best we can while they're having a problem. And that's an awesome responsibility. I'm not sure worthwhile is the word I am looking for. I think what I really want to say is that we make a difference. The people we work for are probably the most exposed they will ever be in their lives. They are vulnerable.

"We come into their homes or businesses at all hours of the day and night. When we show up, they're having an emergency. Generally, it's when they don't have time to get dressed, do their hair, and show a happy face. They are in pain or out of touch with normal life. If you can show me someone having a normal day while watching his or her house burn, I would be surprised."

The captain went on. "People know when they dial that magic number, they will get service quickly. They expect us to do whatever we can to help. While we're not always successful, we pride ourselves on helping in any way we can. Isn't that why you're here?"

"Yes."

"We practice," the captain continued, "so that when we get the call, we're efficient and get the job done quickly with little thought to schedules or the daily grind. We perform miracles every day. People, often at this vulnerable time, trust us to make the best decisions to make their lives better. That relationship has been built over the last 200 years, and it's our job to protect that heritage."

Just then the Healthcare Flywheel began spinning in my head. *Did the fire chief pick these individuals so I could learn about the flywheel?* I asked myself. The captain had hit on the values that kept it from spinning off its center. Purpose, Worthwhile Work, and Making a Difference. He obviously had a passion for the job.

"Captain, how do you keep this all in perspective?"

Chapter 5: Purpose, Worthwhile Work, Making a Difference

"By keeping my priorities straight. When we're in the firehouse, our first responsibility is to make sure we respond to people's emergencies quickly and efficiently. That means making sure our gear is ready to go. That's why I asked you to put your gear by the truck. If we need to respond, I want to make sure my crew is ready and we're out the door to help in seconds, not minutes. People's lives depend upon those seconds. Let's make those seconds count.

"By establishing priorities, we get our jobs done by working as a team. Each member of the team strives to accomplish the goals established by the leader, whoever he or she is. Take, for instance, when we respond to a medical emergency. Who sets the priorities on the call?"

"The paramedic," I responded.

"Are you sure?" the captain asked.

"Of course. The paramedic assesses the patient's signs and symptoms, and acts as the eyes and ears for the doctor at the Emergency Department," I said proudly.

"I guess that's one way of looking at it," the captain said. "My point is, you had to assess the symptoms of the patient. So the patient's body was telling you the priorities."

"Well, from that perspective, you're right. But who sets the priorities for the crew on the call?" I asked.

"The paramedic. Sounds like a war of words. I wanted you to see that there are other perspectives that officers need to be aware of."

"I hadn't thought of it that way. Guess it's like my parents always said, 'There are two sides to every story.'"

Just then a voice yelled from the kitchen, "Gumbo's hot—come and get it before it gets cold."

"Perfect timing. This looks like a good place to take a break and 'digest' what we've been talking about," the captain said.

"Thanks, Captain Fletcher," I said with a chuckle. "I appreciate your time."

"You're welcome. If you need help after you finally get promoted, give me a call. Now let's eat."

It's amazing to see firefighters when they sit down to lunch! Just like a big family. You could close your eyes and see someone passing the rice while another was scooping potato salad. The chatter around the table was this and that, catching up on old times—only they hadn't seen each other for a mere two days. After the meal, each person helped with the cleanup. That's when Chief O'Reilly arrived.

He and Captain Fletcher went back to the captain's office for a few minutes, and then the chief called out, "Hey, Benjamin, time to hit the road. Grab your gear."

I thanked everyone for their hospitality, collected my equipment, and headed for the door. The chief was not far behind.

CHAPTER SIX

THE FLYWHEEL'S PRINCIPLES

I spent the afternoon driving Chief O'Reilly from one firehouse to the next. At each place, the same routine took place. Say hi to everyone, sit down, listen to what's happening in their lives, and then meet with the officer. Not every firehouse had a captain supervising the crew. In most, a lieutenant worked closely with a crew of three or four others. Captains were in strategically located firehouses since they were responsible for the supervision of other lieutenants and any major alarms in their respective areas.

As we traveled the district, I came to appreciate Chief O'Reilly's style of management. His was a method that allowed interaction with the crews. Yet when he needed to, he commanded authority as someone who had earned his "stripes," as they say. Chief O'Reilly was the guy in town who heard everyone's stories and kept everyone's secrets. He helped whenever possible and constantly encouraged people.

After visiting five other firehouses, we made a stop at the administration building.

"This should be a quick stop, kid. Don't get too involved here. We gotta be in and out."

"Right, Chief," was all I managed to say before he was out of the vehicle. I followed him, but at his pace I had a hard time keeping up. I almost ran to the entrance door to open it before he could get there.

Sounds silly now, but I wanted to observe Chief O'Reilly every step of the way.

As he entered the building, he greeted almost everyone within earshot by name. And everyone returned a smile and a greeting. I was lucky to remember half their names.

Just then, he turned to me and said, "Kid, gotta meet with the chief. Make yourself comfortable, keep an ear to the radio, and meet me in the truck in case we get a call."

"Yes, Chief," I replied. At that I walked down the hall to get a drink from the break room. I remembered that the last time I was in here, I was learning about the Healthcare Flywheel. Now I was seeing its effects in every firehouse, every person, and in every situation. *What was it Chief Black said?* I asked myself. *Oh yeah—Purpose, Worthwhile Work, and Making a Difference are the hub. Passion, Principles, and Pillar Results make the wheel turn.* I was beginning to feel like I had just scratched the surface. I understood the passion and hub concepts. I was seeing it in everything I was doing today. I wondered if Chief Black had anything on the principles I could read while I waited.

A Walking Encyclopedia

I quickly moved down the hall to Chief Black's office, but the outer door was closed. The division secretary asked if she could help. *What was her name?* I asked myself. *Sandy! That's it.*

I stammered, "Uh, yes. I was going to see if Chief Black had some specific material about the Healthcare Flywheel. She's been helping me understand how it fits into the officer development program. Do you know when she'll be back?"

"She's gone the rest of the day. State EMS coordinating committee," Sandy answered. "If you like, I can send her an email and ask her when she can meet with you."

"No, I was just in the building and thought I'd stop by. Thanks just the same."

Chapter 6: The Flywheel's Principles

"Perhaps I can help you?" she asked.

"That'd be great! I was looking for information on how the principles work with the flywheel," I said, not expecting Sandy to know what I was talking about.

"Not a problem," she said. "If you have a few minutes, I can explain a little about how this works.

"You know, of course, about the individual parts of the flywheel, how they fit together, what makes the wheel spin, and how the spin is sustained and then how energy is created—don't you?" Sandy asked.

I was floored. Sandy was the EMS division's secretary, and here she was, a walking encyclopedia on the Healthcare Flywheel.

"Well, yes I do." *How did she know so much?* "But I was specifically looking for the next step. I'm not sure exactly how long I have, though. When Chief O'Reilly is done with the fire chief, I need to leave. I'm his assigned driver today," I said with pride.

"Sit down and make yourself comfortable until you have to leave," she told me. "I have the material you need right here."

Sandy Baker looked to be in her mid-thirties. Blonde hair, green eyes, and a slender build, I thought she was probably a little under five foot eight. I'd heard through the grapevine she knew where all of the skeletons were hidden. Rumor also had it that Sandy had been here almost 20 years. That would mean she must have been in high school when she started.

She pulled out her copy of the Healthcare Flywheel, the same as the one I'd been given. But her copy was on slightly yellowed paper, and the edges had seen better days. She must have had it for some time.

"I assume Elle gave you a copy of this?" she asked.

"Elle?" I looked at her quizzically.

"Sorry, the chief and I work so closely together, sometimes I forget you guys don't use first names. I meant Chief Black." Sandy looked down at the paper in front of her as she took out a pencil. "We're a little less formal here than in the field. You can call me Sandy if you like. I would prefer it. I keep thinking Ms. Baker sounds like a school teacher. But, I guess that's what I am today. Right?"

"If you say so," I said with a smile.

"So, let me get this straight. Chief Black has explained how the flywheel spins on center and begins to move. Right?"

"Yes, ma'am." Now it was my turn to be a little more formal. I was beginning to think I had underestimated Sandy Baker.

"You know what keeps us centered, and what makes the wheel spin. Now let's look at how the spin is sustained." She took her pencil and pointed at the principles section on the flywheel.

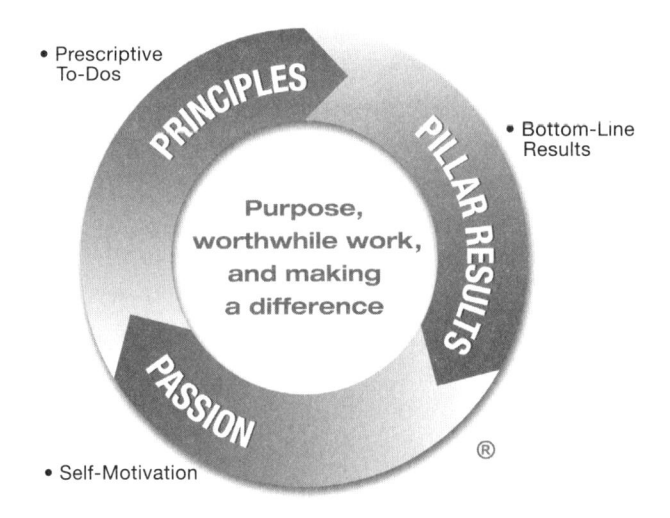

- Prescriptive To-Dos

PRINCIPLES

PILLAR RESULTS

- Bottom-Line Results

Purpose, worthwhile work, and making a difference

PASSION

- Self-Motivation

®

"Sometimes we call these 'Prescriptive To-Dos.' They're principles that help create a great culture and get the results we're after. But they also help sustain the passion that started the flywheel turning to begin with. You can be a man of great passion, but if it isn't fed and sustained, eventually it will die out. It's the same with the wheel. It slows unless the passion is nurtured, but it turns faster as the passion drives the implementation of the principles that drive results. These results further fuel the passion, and the flywheel spins faster.

"It has little to do with who you are or what you do. It has everything to do with who you want to be and where you want to go. I know this sounds confusing, but when I first heard about it from Quint Studer, it took me a little time to understand it, too."

Chapter 6: The Flywheel's Principles

"Chief Black said she heard it from Mr. Studer as well."

"Yes, she did. When I told Elle about Mr. Studer's program *Taking You and Your Organization to the Next Level,* and that he was speaking at a conference on the future of healthcare, she was intrigued. She mentioned it to the fire chief, and the rest is history."

"Not to get off the subject, but would you be willing to be one of the people I study for the officer orientation?"

Surprised, Sandy looked me straight in the eye and said, "I don't really know what I have to offer!"

"A lot, I think. You know about the Healthcare Flywheel because you've been through how it was introduced here, and you live it. You can add a new dimension to how all this works."

"For that, young man, you'll have to make an appointment."

"Fair enough."

"All right, let's look at the principles." As she was talking, she pulled out a plain sheet of paper. She numbered the paper from one at the top, under the words "Healthcare Flywheel Principles," to nine near the bottom of the page.

The Prescriptive To-Dos

"The nine principles are easy." She began to write. "First up is commit to excellence. Second, measure the important things. Third, build a culture around service. Fourth, create and develop leaders. Fifth, focus on employee satisfaction. Sixth, build individual accountability. Seventh, align behaviors with goals and values. Eighth, communicate at all levels. And last, but certainly one of the most important things, recognize and reward success."

She handed me the piece of paper on which she had neatly written:

> # Healthcare Flywheel
> ## Principles/"Prescriptive To-Dos"
> 1. Commit to Excellence
> 2. Measure the Important Things
> 3. Build a Culture Around Service
> 4. Create and Develop Leaders
> 5. Focus on Employee Satisfaction
> 6. Build Individual Accountability
> 7. Align Behaviors with Goals and Values
> 8. Communicate at All Levels
> 9. Recognize and Reward Success

"Do you see anything on this sheet that we don't already do?" she asked. "I want you to take this list. If you do see something we aren't doing or something you feel we can do better, please let me know. I make it my job to keep this flywheel turning."

"Really? Why is it your responsibility?" I asked.

"Each of us is responsible for keeping it turning. Not just me, not just you. All of us. But it has to start with one. And then another, and another. Until the wheel is turning with such momentum you would be hard pressed to stop it with one bad day, one bad call, or one bad employee."

Wow, I thought. *She is passionate about this organization. But she's just a secretary!* I would have to find out more about Ms. Sandy Baker.

"Can you tell me about…"

"Come on, kid, got things to do," interrupted Chief O'Reilly. "Afternoon, Sandy. Thanks for babysitting."

I jumped to my feet. "Thank you, Ms. Baker. I appreciate your time. And thanks for the list!" I said.

"Sure, any help I can give you, please call."

I picked up the paper with the list on it, stuffed it in my pocket, and hustled to catch up to the battalion chief.

TACTICAL CONSIDERATIONS

The Nine Principles keep the flywheel spinning. They consist of techniques, tools, and behaviors proven to achieve results and help you meet your goals. These guiding principles focus on specific actions that will have the greatest impact on your organization. The chapters ahead explain in detail what each of these "Prescriptive To-Dos" is all about.

CHAPTER SEVEN

COMMIT TO EXCELLENCE

The Training Center

Chief O'Reilly really was in a hurry. He said he'd drive. I had no idea where we were going until we arrived at the Metro Fire Training Center, established to prepare and educate fire and rescue personnel from around the area. Four fire departments joined together and purchased the land, each one paying a percentage of the cost to build a classroom/office building, a maze, a burn building, and a tower.

At the time, the leaders responsible for the center had vision. They built a state-of-the-art facility with gas burners instead of pallets and hay, as well as incident simulators. It has a changeable maze. After a crew uses it, a few panels are moved around, making it a whole new experience for the next exercise. A collapse rescue simulator and confined space area have been added. Propane car fires can be fought; there's a train car, and even an aircraft prop. A pad for auto extrication exercises was constructed, and a town was built to scale, which the police department uses as well.

The last time I was here I was learning to drive the fire engines. There is a section where streets are marked out on the pavement with traffic signs and parking areas to practice backing the truck. The area even has a stop-and-go traffic light. All of this is computer controlled

Frontline Heroes: A Story of Saving Lives

from a tower right beside the classroom facility—the building for which we were headed.

As we pulled up, Chief O'Reilly told me that I would be meeting with Captain Ira J. Storm. He didn't just say Ira Storm; he said Ira J. Storm. 'Course, I knew exactly who he was talking about. Captain Storm was a veteran of the fire service. He'd been around as long as anyone could remember and had worked with one of the smaller departments for many years before he got the bug to check out emergency medical services one day. He liked it so much he left his department and jumped right into the position of EMS chief of our department. He eventually worked his way up the chain of command to become the fire chief.

That was 15 years ago. Rumor had it that when he retired, they asked him to teach a class or two at the new fire training center. He ended up staying, except now he's called "captain" and he runs the place.

Captain Storm prides himself on the center, and a big plaque his wife made still graces the front door. It reads, "Through these doors pass the greatest Americans—firefighters, emergency medical practitioners, rescue workers, and those who'd give their lives so others may live."

This is one facility to which I know the other fire chiefs fear to come unless they have Captain Storm's permission and they follow "his" rules. If you violate them, you'll never come back. I've heard stories about a guy who told the captain that rules were meant to be broken, and he never returned. I think he moved out of state. It's not that Captain Storm is an imposing man—he stands approximately five foot 10 inches tall, 250 pounds, a little round about the middle, with a growl that would scare a mountain lion. But mainly he's soft-spoken with a cheerful smile below his heavy, "old school" mustache he loves to massage into place whenever he's deep in thought.

Chief O'Reilly broke into my thoughts. "Kid, I've got to go handle somethin' while you do your interview. I'll be back shortly."

"Sure, Chief," I said. I barely had time to get my gear out of the vehicle before he sped away.

Chapter 7: Commit to Excellence

Just outside the door to the classroom building was an area for gear storage. The sign read, "NO bunker gear in the building—that means YOU." I stored my equipment in a locker and proceeded into the building. The hallway was lined with class pictures going back to the very beginning. Custom-made flags that represented the class's ideals were hung directly above the pictures. Each was different. Some had eagles; others had a skull and crossbones like pirates. Some had the star of life and still others the ol' standby—the Maltese cross. Each of them either had a motto, like "Carpe Diem," or an image such as a firefighter shooting a fire stream towards a dragon emblazoned with "Innovate, Adapt, and Overcome." Okay, it sounds corny, but I was looking for that one. It was our academy motto, since our instructors kept telling us to "think outside the box."

These were fond memories now, yet at the time it seemed like anything but. I remember the fire academy like it was yesterday, thinking it would never end. The instructors pounded us with physical training and agility exercises. The training required you to carry a 180-pound mannequin down a four-story tower in full firefighter gear. Once you got to the bottom, you had to take off your gear and give 15 minutes of cardio pulmonary resuscitation to a "victim." And then came running—which at first we thought was a joke. Why should we run a mile and a half in under 15 minutes? We don't run on the "scene." As a matter of fact, we'd probably get disciplined for running. But we understood why we had to run after the first six weeks, when we did our first rescue and found out how important it was to have stamina and how a healthy body could prevent a heart attack.

I also reminisced about how close we became as a class. Some nights, we would go to a "dive" called the Ground Pound. It was a restaurant that sometimes had live music we'd listen to, or we'd go just to laugh and enjoy a drink on the patio overlooking the river. We didn't know anything about being firefighters, but we thought we did, and we could tell good stories. Now my reminiscence made it seem like fun. Back then, however… Anyway, those are the people I still contact. I am proud of our class, and I was glad to see the picture in the hall.

Stormy's Story

I came to the end of the first floor hallway. There was a Dutch door with a small ledge dividing the top and bottom halves. The top half was open. On the ledge sat a small silver bell accompanied by a Post-it note that read "Ring bell for service."

Okay, I thought. *Let's see what happens.* I rang the bell. I didn't hear any rustling from inside the office. I waited a couple of minutes, and tapped the bell several more times.

"Hold yer horses," came a voice. I heard a door creaking shut. "Watcha need?"

"Captain Storm, my name is Frank Benjamin. I'm here to talk to you today? I had an appointment this morning?" Totally unsure of myself, I sounded like I was guessing at everything I said.

"Why sure, come on in." Captain Storm opened the door and let me enter. "Give me a minute and we can talk in my office." He showed me the way, and as I entered his office, I half-expected to see more photographs of past fire academies. Instead, I came face to face with pictures of Captain Storm shaking hands with the president of the United States and the secretary of the Department of Homeland Security, photos of him testifying before Congress, and other pictures about which I could only guess. I saw photographs of the captain's family on his desk, his filing cabinet, and on the wall. These had been taken in exotic locales such as Tahiti, the Caribbean, the Arctic Circle, even on K2, a mountain that looks like the Matterhorn in the Disney movies but is the second highest mountain on earth.

"Sorry about that," Captain Storm said, breaking my sense of wonderment as he entered the room. "Had to get some of the soot off my hands. So, how can I help you?"

What an eye-opener! I thought I'd been sent to talk to the training guru, but instead here I was in the presence of a man who'd met with kings, so to speak. I was fascinated. He might have a background as a fire service professional who'd been a fire chief and was now known simply as "captain," but he utilized a rich life experience as head of this training center!

"Captain Storm, it is such a pleasure to meet you. My fire chief gave us an assignment—people we're to interview as a part of our officer orientation program. Your name was on my list. I apologize for not making our scheduled appointment time—we had a call."

"Not a problem; the training center is pretty quiet today. Guess that means the quiet before the storm, as they say," he commented, laughing.

It took me a second or two to get the joke.

"Captain, I should probably mention I'm not sure how much time I have. My ride is Chief O'Reilly. He had to go take care of business and didn't need me for a little while."

"No problem. However, calling me 'Captain' seems like overkill. Please…for today, it's Stormy."

I felt a level of comfort in Stormy's presence that I hadn't experienced thus far in my interviews. He didn't stand on ceremony, for one thing. I believed I could tell him anything and he would safeguard my secrets. I sat back, not afraid to ask any of the questions I had prepared…but now they seemed so inadequate.

"Stormy," I said, feeling weird because of the lack of ceremony, "why do you think it was important for the fire chief to assign me interviews as a part of the officer development program? But, before you answer, let me ask…couldn't I have gained the same information from reading?"

"Frankly, I think the interview is a great idea. Sure, you could read a book. Look around you. I've read all the books on my shelves, some of them twice, some of them 20 or 30 times."

I saw stacks of books in a nearby closet, some old with leather bindings and others that looked new.

"But," he continued, "I've learned that books give you only part of the picture. They don't give you the look on a person's face when he tells you something, how he feels about it, the position of his body. If people are excited by something, their bodies tell part of the story.

"It's the human interaction that's important in an interview. It teaches you so many things. Respect for the person you are interviewing, or for the interviewer. How to formulate questions and structure them to gain insight and information. It also builds trust between people. Remember, the interviewee is trusting that the information obtained will be used for good purposes and not to rip apart what that person has worked hard to attain."

I must have had an intense expression on my face as I said, "That adds a lot of insight."

"I think that your taking this assignment as seriously as you are indicates you want to be the best at what you do, and offer the best to the department. That, my good man, is an indicator that the fire chief—as the Templar knight in *Indiana Jones* would say—'chose wisely.'"

The Department's Greatest Asset

"Thank you. Stormy, I've been asking everyone about the Healthcare Flywheel. I understand how the hub makes the wheel turn steadily and on center, and I understand how passion gets the wheel turning. I met with Sandy Baker, who wrote down a list of the principles she called the 'Prescriptive To-Dos.'"

I took it out of my pocket and handed it to Stormy. "But I'm not certain what the principles do to actually make the wheel spin."

"Easy enough, but it will take a lot of time to explain each one in detail. I could make a whole college-level class out of that one. So, you've met the greatest asset your department has?"

Confused, I looked at him and said, "Greatest asset?"

"Sure, do you know who Ms. Sandy Baker is?"

"She's the EMS division secretary," I answered without hesitation.

"Partially. Sandy is responsible for most of what your department is credited with today. She is a mover and a shaker. Sandy was the first female paramedic in our state's history. She earned her nursing degree with honors from the university. She gave up her fire department job to

Chapter 7: Commit to Excellence

develop one of the first regional aeromedical helicopter programs. She knew James Page from the Los Angeles Fire Department and Doctor Jarvis personally. Even gets invited to dinner when they are in town. It was said she could pick up the phone and call them, and they would drop whatever they were doing to take her call. She helped set up the protocols for fire-based EMS, not just here, but nationally. That lady will never tell you what she has done or why, but she has a history, and she'd be a great ally for you."

I was flabbergasted. "Then why is she just a secretary?" I asked.

"Don't ever believe anyone is 'just a secretary.' We all have hopes and dreams. Perhaps being a secretary fits better into that person's world. Sandy Baker is a perfect example. There she was, an up-and-coming certified emergency nurse, with doctors asking her for advice. Then one day she gave it all up."

"Why? Sounds to me like a dream job!" I said.

"It was—until her priorities changed. You see, she met someone while doing all this work. A wonderful man she married and had kids with. She planned on spending the rest of her life in his company. One day, all that ended in tragedy. He was killed. Afterwards, she decided her job took her away from what mattered the most—her children. So Sandy quit the long hours and took a job working from home until the kids were in school. When she tried to get a job with the fire department again, she was told she was too old to hire as a paramedic on an engine company."

"Too old?" I said. "She can't even be 40 yet."

"Ah, the voice of youth. Sandy Baker is in the second half of her forties. But she had a lot to give to the fire and rescue service when she came back. Since the fire department didn't have any openings, your fire chief came to me and told me what a gem he'd found and that he just needed to find a position for her until he could hire her. Remember, at the time, he was not the fire chief. I had heard about Sandy from a few of my friends and talked the board into hiring her here at the training center. I knew full well your fire chief would find her a job with the department. Well, she worked for me for about two years, developing our training program. She was a great instructor and we wanted to have her teach full-time. Her priorities, however, were elsewhere. She wanted 'regular' hours so that she could be with her children when they were home from school. That was her priority then, and it is today. As a matter of fact, her oldest is graduating from high school this spring."

"After he graduates, do you think she will go back into EMS?"

"Not likely, as she'll still have a son and daughter at home. But look at what she can do for you. She has a wealth of knowledge and is willing to share. Why don't you interview her?"

"I asked if I could. We didn't have much time to talk because Chief O'Reilly came back to bring me here," I said.

"Well, why don't you and your wife invite her out to dinner?" Stormy asked.

How did he know I was married? Did he know more about me than he was letting on? "How do you know about Lexi?" I asked.

"Do you think your fire chief would allow me to be unprepared for our meeting? Besides, the ring on your left hand is a dead giveaway unless you're just trying to scare away the ladies," he laughed.

"Wow, we've really gotten off on a tangent. So, what about the 'Prescriptive To-Dos'?"

The First Principle

"Right," he said. "The 'Prescriptive To-Dos.' You're asking how they bring about a good fire department?"

I nodded.

"These principles don't make a good department," Stormy said. "They can't."

Just as I was about to say something, Stormy raised his eyebrows to stop me. "People make a great department. These are just tools that PEOPLE need and use to make a good department great."

"Oh," I said under my breath. I looked at the list again.

Chapter 7: Commit to Excellence

Healthcare Flywheel
Principles/"Prescriptive To-Dos"

1. Commit to Excellence
2. Measure the Important Things
3. Build a Culture Around Service
4. Create and Develop Leaders
5. Focus on Employee Satisfaction
6. Build Individual Accountability
7. Align Behaviors with Goals and Values
8. Communicate at All Levels
9. Recognize and Reward Success

"You, young man," Stormy went on, "already have a commitment to excellence. It shows in how seriously you're taking your assignments in the officer development program. It shows in that you were chosen over others who took the promotion test, because you studied and worked hard to gain the skills you needed to get in the door. It shows because someone felt you did a great job as a firefighter or paramedic and recommended you to the Promotion Board. So I don't really think we need to discuss how important the first item—commit to excellence—is. Do you?"

I guess I hesitated just a little too long. Stormy said, "I guess you do."

I replied, "I can see it in me, but I don't see it in a lot of others I work with. I tend to gravitate to those who are positive and work hard to make this department the best. Others just want to get through the day and get the paycheck. Wouldn't that frustrate you?" I asked.

"Now you're seeing why you and your colleagues in the officer development program were given the Healthcare Flywheel. It can be utilized by an individual, group, or organization. Your chief is smart enough to know that babies take tentative steps at first, but once they get the hang of it, they are walking all over the house. Nothing different here. Except the baby steps for the department were to get the executives on board. The fire chief has already done that. Can you name one chief officer who isn't committed to excellence?"

I shook my head "no." I couldn't think of any. Not that I knew too many, but those I did—Chief Black for instance—were committed to excellence.

"This is not…shall we say…a 'flavor of the month program.' It is the foundation of what the fire chief and his team are trying to do. If each person does not care about excellence in his or her own life and work, then there is no point in continuing to the next step. It is just *that* important. It's vital to the journey you are beginning. If you cannot commit to excellence, then I don't need to be speaking with you today."

Now I'd done it. He was mad at me. How do I get the interview back on track? I asked myself. *I'll just switch to the next question.* "How do you define excellence?" I asked Stormy.

"Excellence is experienced when people feel valued. When our customers feel the service and quality they are receiving is extraordinary. Let me ask you, why do you attend continuing education for paramedicine?"

"So that I can keep up on the latest techniques and improvements in EMS," I stated bluntly.

"I'm not asking for me; I am asking you to examine why you do it. I know how important continuing education is for the job. I'm always taking classes and learning."

Chapter 7: Commit to Excellence

"You? But, why you? You've probably forgotten more about fire and rescue than most of us have ever learned."

"Frank, listen to me. You just said that I have 'probably forgotten more than most have ever learned.' I don't want to forget when someone's life is on the line. Here in the training center, it happens on a daily basis, every time we light a fire. A commitment to excellence positively impacts not only the bottom line—it is a must if we are to provide quality fire service on the job as well. It impacts all our member departments, helping each one…how did Studer say it…'live out its mission and values.' You have to commit to excellence or the rest is just some words on a piece of paper.

"Now that I have said all that…These principles go hand-in-hand with the Five Pillars of Excellence: Service, Quality, People, Finance, and Growth. But before we go any further, it's important for you to know how your fire chief is impacted every day when it comes to the pillars. For instance, if you provide poor service, the customers complain. Who do they complain to? The fire chief. If you waste money, who has to explain why you spent x number of dollars on, say, toilet paper? The fire chief.

"When we're all committed to excellence under each of the pillars, there are fewer complaints. This gives the fire chief more time to work on improving our operations. Even little improvements pay dividends to the organization as a whole, eventually lifting us to another level of service to our customers."

"So, what you are saying is that little improvements, even at my level, pay dividends to the organization as a whole, eventually lifting us to another level?"

"I think you're getting the hang of this. Can we go on? I know you're short on time."

I looked at my watch. We had been talking 25 minutes. I expected each interview to last about 15 minutes. But what Stormy was telling me had such an enormous impact, I couldn't end it now. I needed to know more.

TACTICAL CONSIDERATIONS

Commitment to Excellence is about more than the emergency services you provide. It's how you live your daily life. You need to have a plan of attack and believe in that plan if you are to be successful in your commitment. This will require you to take action on whatever goals you have. Professionally, it might mean working towards a college degree or reading whatever you can get your hands on. Personally, it might mean spending quality time with family and friends.

Commitment is also an attitude. With the right attitude, nothing is impossible.

As Captain Storm told Frank, "If each person does not care about excellence in his or her own life and work, then there is no point in continuing to the next step. It is just *that* important. It's vital to the journey you are beginning."

If you cannot commit to excellence, the organization and you will be no different from what you are today.

While the journey will be different for each organization, this chapter set forth some proven tools to bring about change and carry you to a level of greatness.

1. Align the organization into operational pillars (Service, Quality, People, Finance, and Growth) that provide a foundation for setting organizational goals and a direction for service and operational excellence. They also provide consistency and focus over time, helping the team overcome the "newest fad program" barrier.
2. Establish goals below each of the operational pillars.

Remember—little improvements, even at the lowest levels, pay dividends to the entire organization, eventually lifting it to another level of service.

CHAPTER EIGHT

MEASUREMENT AND CULTURE

The Important Things

My interview with Stormy continued. "Okay, what's number two on your list?" he asked.

I looked at the sheet of paper and read, "Number two—measure the important things."

"Measuring results—if you don't know where you are, how do you know where you are going?" Stormy said.

"But it says measure the important things! What *are* the important things?" I blurted out.

"Have you ever been in an organization that measures only what time you show up for work, what time you take your break, how long you were gone, and then what time you went home?"

"Sure, when I was in high school as a bagger at the local grocery store. I hated that job," I said forcefully.

"Keeping that job in mind, would it have been different if your manager had told you how important you were to the operation of the store? How you helped customers by carrying their bags out to their cars? And because of this great service, the store had return customers, which in turn gave you the job?

"Would it have been different if the focus was not on how much time you put in, but on the outstanding service you gave the customer?"

"Sure it would have. But who wants to take the time to talk to a kid? Anyway, I guess I could have been a better bagger."

"What we are missing was measuring what was important in that job. Someone measured your time while you were there, and someone else measured what you got accomplished, or your productivity. The focus was not on what a great service you provided the customer; the focus was on measuring how much time you worked."

"So how do you interpret 'measure the important things'?" I asked.

"Let's turn the tables. What's important to you on the job?" Stormy said, taking out a piece of paper.

"How fast we get out the door. How soon we arrive on the scene of an emergency. How quickly we can evaluate the patient and get that person to more definitive care."

"Those are important operational issues with regard to patient care, are they not?" Stormy asked.

"Of course. If the patient hasn't been breathing for six minutes or more, we could be facing additional complications or brain damage."

"Excellent, so you are measuring things that are important. But what about a fire call? What difference does it make if it takes fifteen minutes instead of five?"

Before I could say anything, Stormy said, "You needn't answer that. I know the difference is containing the fire to room of origin versus having to fight to save the rest of the house. But I want you to concentrate on measuring important things. Response times and incident reports help us to improve our service. Most of the time, we look to these reports to save us in case of a lawsuit. But can't they also be used to assist us in service improvement?"

"I hadn't looked at it that way before." I always thought fire reports were a pain to write, and so did most everyone else. The EMS reports, though, were our best accounting of what we actually did to save the life of a patient. The narratives provided who, what, when, where, and how we did it. Some were actually interesting and amazing. I remembered reading about a paramedic who had to establish a line on a patient trapped in a ditch, upside down in a car. The patient's arm was pinned under the car and the medic had to find a vein in the dark, in freezing temperatures, after wading through standing water in the ditch. Later we found out he had to keep the patient's head out of the water or the patient would have drowned. All this while trying to get an IV established.

Fire reports could give us similar value. They gave us the data to show what we did and why we did it. I was beginning to see what "measure the important things" meant.

"When clear goals are combined with consistent measurement and aligned behaviors, results are soon to follow. It is important to have measurement practices in place as well as methods to see if the outcomes meet the goals of the team, unit, or organization," Stormy explained.

"I think I get it. We do this on every fire. We have clearly defined goals for our team, everyone operating at the scene. The entire incident is managed through the incident commander or operations chief. We have certain benchmarks we hit—like 'primary search complete,' or even 'rescue complete, extension stopped, fire contained, fire extinguished, overhaul completed.' So what you are saying is that these benchmarks are one method of measuring what is important. On the fire ground, we focus on these. In the firehouse, we focus on others."

"Correct," Stormy said.

Just then I heard a vehicle pull up outside the building. I was hoping it wasn't Chief O'Reilly. We had gotten to only the second principle, with seven more on the list. There was a lot more to it than I had thought there would be.

Focus on Service

"What about number three—build a culture around service? So far we have created goals by committing to excellence and established how we are going to measure the important things. Don't we already have a culture of service?" I asked.

"Yes and no. Why does a hospital need to build a culture of service—doesn't it already provide a service to its customers in the form of healthcare? Yes it does, but there's more to it. Just because someone has to have a heart bypass doesn't mean that they should give up the need for someone who *cares*, who is there to ensure comfort, cleanliness, and good treatment. A culture of service is all about making a difference in the life of the patient.

"And who is the customer, anyway? Aren't employees customers? What about physicians? A culture of service is making sure both internal and external customers are cared for. In your business, who takes care of you?" Stormy asked.

"We take care of each other and we're proud of the fact," I replied. But he knew this. *Why did he ask?*

"Great. But who makes that possible? Before you answer, consider this. The fire chief gives an order for what you'll be doing. This order comes down the chain until it reaches you. But who fights your battles for raises or job security? Who makes sure you are provided with the tools you need to do your job? Who fights for the new fire truck? The fire chief. Yet everyone assumes he's on the other side because he works for the Board of Directors or City Council. So do you.

"And what about the battalion chief? Isn't he an operations employee working 24-hour shifts just like you? Although he doesn't work immediately with someone, he reports to someone. Correct? Who takes care of him? On the fire ground, you take care of him. But what about if he's having a day where he needs an emotional pick-me-up? Who gives it to him? You expect him to give you one, but what about him? What I am trying to show you is that to create service excellence, you go up *and* down the chain—not just down.

"Creating this kind of culture includes getting input from the entire organization, top to bottom. I'll bet when you have a problem in your department, you know the very people who will insist their answer is the only 'right' way to do it. Creating a culture of service includes everyone."

The Construction Crew

Stormy continued. "We learned a long time ago that committees are the death of any good idea. So the term 'service team' has come to prominence. Do you know what service teams are?"

"Not really."

"Service teams are simply what their name indicates. Let's take, for instance, the communication team. This team is responsible for 'connecting the dots' between doing something and what we hope to achieve. This helps all employees understand the reasons for operational excellence. The team also works to improve communication processes by utilizing newsletters, communications boards, pass downs, and so on. Plus, this team works closely with other groups to ensure they're getting *their* messages out. They help tell the story. Can you see how important the communication team is to building a culture of service?" Stormy asked.

"Well," I paused, "sort of! I mean, I understand how important the communication team is to getting the word out. But what does that have to do with creating a culture of service?"

"I guess I put the cart before the horse, as they say. Service teams engage everyone in creating the culture. They provide an opportunity for all employees to be a part of the process. Some people have talents in one area, while others have different things to contribute. But everyone has an equal opportunity to participate in changing the organization from being merely okay to GREAT. And when they see the results, they become even more committed, engaged, and excited.

"A service team can also change something that doesn't work without waiting forever for the organization to get around to it. You know your job—who knows better what needs to be fixed and how to do it?

"I know what you're about to say…and yes, there are those who will not participate unless they're paid for it. That's the first hurdle, but in the beginning they won't be the ones we focus on. Instead, your fire chief will offer highly motivated employees the tools and resources they need to identify and solve key service and operational issues that cross over departments. Am I right?"

"I think that's what we're working on now. The new officer development program might be the first step?"

"Right. There's another reason for service teams. Many times fire chiefs find that employees have good ideas for improvements, but never have the chance to put them into practice. The service teams bring together those ideas and implement them, helping the organization get to the next level. The groups have the structure and permission to do what everyone talks about around the table."

"Okay, I think I understand the concept," I told him. "Let's see. Service teams help create the culture by focusing on an aspect of the organization that is either lacking or in need of improvement."

"Correct," said Stormy.

I went on. "Another key way to focus on service is to engage employees by providing them the opportunity for action that will create results. When they see results, they will more fully understand and thereby become more committed to change. Hey, it's like self-motivation. It helps the flywheel turn."

"Good reasoning. But it's different in a way, since the flywheel is turning already. Isn't it?" Stormy asked.

"It is."

"Then this movement will provide momentum to keep it moving. Remember, we talked about if motivation isn't fed, it can go away. So this is the feeding process."

"So what teams should be formed?" I asked.

"My advice is to look at what you need to accomplish. Once you have evaluated the organization and determined what opportunities you have for improvement, teams will have to develop goals to achieve the needed results. Here, look at this."

With that, Stormy grabbed a piece of paper. Across the top he wrote "service teams," and then he listed them.

<u>SERVICE TEAMS</u>
Standards Team
Customer Satisfaction Team
Employer of Choice Team
Measurement Team
Service Recovery Team
Communication Team
Reward and Recognition Team

Teamwork Defined

"Let me tell you what each of these teams does, just as an example. The standards team is responsible for developing the standards of behavior for all employees when providing service or interacting with one another. The team also develops tools and strategies to ensure everyone lives up to these standards."

He went on to list what some of the other teams strive for.

"Customer satisfaction team—responsible for ensuring the highest level of service is consistently provided and for developing new ideas to continually improve service. This team shares best practices to help others learn.

"Employer of choice team—responsible for helping the organization become *the* preferred employer, a place where everyone feels they're doing worthwhile work, making a difference, and finding purpose in their jobs. This team's efforts can include employee selection and orientation, employee forums, and employee surveys. With all the competition out there, we want to *keep* our people, not train them for someone else.

"Measurement team—responsible for what is measured and why. Team members become data experts and develop user-friendly, easy-to-read reports so that everyone knows the score on a timely basis. They work closely with the satisfaction team to identify trends for improvement. In healthcare and the fire service as well, the measurement data compares the organization against national and locally-developed standards.

"Service recovery team—responsible for developing service recovery policies for those whose expectations have not been met. The group also educates leaders and employees on how to use service recovery tools. The goal is to ensure that when employees learn a problem exists, they do something about it—right then and there.

"Communication team—connecting the dots for employees. Remember, we already talked about this one earlier.

"Reward and recognition team—responsible for developing ideas to build reward and recognition into the daily practices of leaders and employees. Creating instant recognition programs, ensuring leaders are using available programs, and celebrating achievements are just a few of the areas this team works on."

I was writing as fast as I could, and found myself almost taking shorthand to get every thought. *After Chief O'Reilly gets here, I'll have to translate my notes so that I can read them later.*

Stormy finished his list quickly, not spending a lot of time on any one particular service team. I think he wanted to make sure I had an idea of what service teams were all about, but didn't want me to get the idea that these were the only teams we could put together.

Just then I heard a door close and footsteps coming down the hall. I had so much left to discover. I needed more time. A knock sounded on the door.

"Come on in," said Captain Storm. The door opened, and I could see Chief O'Reilly standing outside, smiling.

"He been behaving himself?" he asked.

"He's got a lot of questions, I'd say," Stormy said. "You need him back? Or do you want to leave him here? I've got a few things he can do. Only thing is, it's not shift work," he chuckled, implying I could work at the training center full-time.

"I'd better get him back to the station. All this sitting around sharing war stories will make him think he doesn't have to work for a living."

With that, I got up to go. I extended my hand, shook Captain Storm's, and said, "Thanks for the insight. I appreciate your time."

"Call if you have any questions or need help with the rest of the principles!"

"Thanks again." We headed for the battalion chief's vehicle.

TACTICAL CONSIDERATIONS

Measure the Important Things is a diagnostic tool to learn if you are successful at what you're attempting to accomplish and to improve processes. Measurement aligns the team. When clear goals are combined with results, people understand the need for measurement.

"Measuring results—if you don't know where you are, how do you know where you are going?" Stormy asked.

1. Determine and communicate what and why you are measuring. When employees know they're working towards a purposeful goal, chances are they'll spend more quality time on their tasks or strive to improve.

2. Set clear goals for the level you need to reach. Make the targets realistic, quantifiable, and achievable. Don't make

them too big—but big enough for the organization to grow or reach a new level. Baby steps first, then learn to run.

3. Interpret the data. Determine if the group has accomplished its goals. If so, move to the next level by establishing more goals. If not, perform a post mortem to determine why the team fell short. Was it because of people, tools, systems, or barriers? Don't be afraid to determine if the goal simply was not possible because the time available to reach it was too short.

4. Connect the results back to purpose. This allows everyone to share in the successes and failures. Teams learn from both. Don't forget what your purpose is, and ground your organization on it.

Build a Culture Around Service. In the first two principles, we determined that everyone wants to be a part of an excellent organization. We set our goals and established how we are going to find out if we met them.

"Creating a culture of service includes getting input from the entire organization, not just the top, the middle, or the bottom." Establish service teams to allow all members to participate. People will have differing levels and types of expertise to contribute.

The key to driving process improvement is to focus on one area at a time. By building service teams that concentrate on specific areas concurrently, the culture of the organization can change rapidly and simultaneously.

1. Service teams help the organization incorporate employee ideas for solutions—what everyone talks about around the

water cooler. The ideas are mainstreamed faster and become an accepted part of the structure more quickly.

2. Allow service teams to create results. When they see results, they will become more committed to change and excellence.

3. Institute *Key Words at Key Times*. This can vary greatly by organization. In EMS, it can mean asking your patients, "Do you have any questions about what I am going to do?" Many times, they will not be able to talk to you. However, when you take time to communicate, you end up removing a level of their fear and apprehension.

In fire situations, let the victim of the fire know what you are doing and why. Overhaul can be a scary thing when you don't know why firefighters are doing more damage than was caused by the fire. Communicate with the fire victim what you are doing by searching for hidden fires. The homeowner can then rest assured there will be no additional damage from hidden fires or hazards. As soon as possible, you will get them in to see exactly what damage has occurred so they can begin the healing process.

CHAPTER NINE

A CHANCE TO PRACTICE

"Respond to an Accident with Injuries"

My head was swimming with all that Captain Storm had given me. I was beginning to feel overwhelmed again. *Gotta stick with baby steps until I learn to walk*, I reminded myself.

The drive was pretty quiet. I didn't ask the battalion chief where he went, nor did he ask what Captain Storm and I had talked about. I clumsily deciphered my scribbled notes. We listened to the radio and were in our own worlds until dispatch interrupted our thoughts. The alarm tones went off.

"Engine 4, Rescue 2, respond to an accident with injuries at Main and Colorado."

The message was repeated. The location was about six blocks from where we were in traffic. Chief O'Reilly picked up the radio, firmly pressing the button on the microphone, and said, "Communications, this is Battalion 3 responding."

The radio blared, "Battalion 3 responding 1512."

After the chief flipped on the emergency lights and siren, traffic parted so we could get through. A minute later, we arrived at the intersection of Main and Colorado. The chief parked his vehicle to protect the scene from anyone who might not be paying attention to the traffic signal. As soon as he had the vehicle in "park" he looked at me and said, "I'm gonna need your best today, kid! You'll be the medical officer as soon as others get here. Get your gear on and triage the scene."

With that he got on the radio. "Communications, Battalion 3 on scene, Main and Colorado. We have a two-car MVA (multiple vehicle accident) with multiple patients. I will need additional ambulances and another alarm to this location. Please give me a TAC channel (tactical channel). Battalion 3 will be Colorado Command."

Communications repeated back the chief's narrative and assigned TAC Three.

I had my gear on in an instant. My heart was beating like it was in competition with the wail of the sirens. The chief was showing confidence in me by letting me act as his medical officer on scene. As I began to survey the scene, it looked as if no one would survive. I could only hope for the best.

I looked over to my right and saw a teenage boy holding his right arm with blood streaming down his face. A teenage girl who didn't appear to have any outward injuries was crying hysterically. A large mid-80s SUV was lying on its side. The driver's area was intact with major damage to the windshield. The rear of the vehicle that should have had a fiberglass roof was open as if there hadn't been any roof at all. Seconds later, I saw it had landed in a grassy area about 100 feet from where the SUV rested. The engine compartment was extremely damaged. As crunched as it was, it looked like someone had run the vehicle into a building.

A little beyond the SUV were two teenagers. One was lying on her back, not moving, with her right leg twisted at an unnatural angle. The other teenager had a laceration behind her left ear and blood was streaming down the front of her blouse. She was shaking the one lying on the ground, screaming, "Don't die on me, Emily!"

As I came around the back of the SUV, I found four more kids, all of them teenagers: one with his leg pinned beneath the SUV, unconscious; another moaning, writhing in pain on his back. One more, wandering aimlessly in the middle of the street, appeared to be un

Chapter 9: A Chance to Practice

aware of what he was doing. The fourth teenager was holding a piece of bloody cloth on top of a wound of some sort.

About 20 feet away was a smaller car. It had serious damage to the passenger side of the vehicle, with intrusion about three to four feet. If the car had been on its side, it would have looked like a "U" shape. The windshield was heavily starred, indicating either that the driver hit it with his head or that some other object inside the vehicle flew into it. The driver was still strapped into his seat, but the steering wheel appeared out of round, indicating he may have some internal injuries. His head was tilted down towards his chest.

Nine patients, two cars, I thought, preparing my radio report. I took a deep breath and began transmitting. "Command, Medical. I have two cars with major damage and have identified nine patients at this time."

Simple Triage and Rapid Treatment

Command acknowledged the information and I walked over to the car. I pulled the driver's door, but nothing happened. Either it was locked or stuck in the closed position. I reached into the passenger compartment next, to see if that door was locked. It wasn't. I knew it would take some time for a crew with tools to get to this patient. I felt for pulses and breathing. He was alive. Since I was alone, I decided to utilize the START triage system. START stands for "simple triage and rapid treatment." I would be making a rapid assessment of every patient, taking less than a minute per person to determine which category the patient should be in.

This one had good respiration, but his pulse was over 30 a minute. He needed help fast. I didn't have any triage tags with me, but I had some survey tape in two colors, orange and yellow, along with a marker. I had been using these for hose testing, and now they would prove to be extremely useful. I grabbed the driver's arm and tied some orange survey tape to it. On the tape I wrote, "RES-OK, P-30+, 1516."

Okay, I said to myself, *one immediate*. I moved on.

Walking back to the SUV, I got to the girls. I gently grabbed the shoulders of the girl screaming, "Emily!" and turned her around to look at me. "Hey, what's your name?"

"Allison," she said through her tears.

"I need you to work with me right now. I need you to stay with me and do exactly as I say. All right?"

A sniffle, then an "okay" as if talking to the ground.

"Can you walk? Do you have any injuries other than on your head?"

"Yes, I can walk," she replied. "I don't know where I'm hurt, maybe just my head."

I took out a four by four bandage and put it on her laceration. "Come with me and hold this on your cut, okay?"

I took her to the side of the street where the other two teenagers were sitting. On her arm I tied a yellow piece of survey tape. I wrote on it, "Allison, RES-OK, P-29–, PERF 2–, Alert 1517."

"I need you to stay right here and help these two until the next paramedic arrives. Can you do that?"

She nodded, wiping away tears. While I was there, I looked at the first two kids I had seen when we arrived on scene. I asked the boy his name.

"Brad," was the answer.

I asked him if he had any injuries other than his arm.

He said, "No."

I figured he was exhibiting signs of shock, as he didn't realize he had blood running down his face. I took out another dressing and asked the girl if she had any injuries.

She said she didn't think so, but Brad was her boyfriend and she was afraid he was going to die.

"We're gonna work hard to make sure everyone gets taken care of. But I need your help. Can you hold this dressing on his head until another paramedic gets here?" I asked. She nodded, took the dressing, and gingerly placed it on Brad's forehead. I tied a yellow piece of survey tape on her after I took her vitals. On her tape I wrote, "RES-OK, P-29–, PERF 2–, Alert 1519."

I ran through Brad's vitals. I took out another piece of tape, this time orange. On it I printed, "RES-OK, P-29–, PERF 2+, Alert 1519."

As I was about to move to the next patient, I asked Brad's girlfriend, "Can you take care of Allison and Brad? I really need your help."

She nodded. As I was about to walk away, she asked, "What do the different colors mean?"

"It's our way of making sure all of you get help. Can you take care of these two for me?"

"Okay," was all I heard as I turned to go to the next patient.

I could hear the arrival of Rescue 2, followed closely by Engine 4. I knew Engine 4 would take a little time getting set up to control the scene, establish fire control, and stabilize the cars. Rescue 2 would be talking with command first, then following my triage. That meant they'd be handling the orange tagged patients first.

As I got to the unconscious girl, I felt for a pulse. *Good, she has pulses*, I thought to myself. I remembered her name was Emily.

"Emily…can you talk to me?" There was no response. I checked for capillary refill and then tagged her with orange survey tape: "Emily, RES-OK, P-29–, PERF 2–, 1520."

I didn't need to move her. This would help incoming units identify treatment needs when they got there.

"Command, Medical. I have three orange and two yellow. One orange is trapped in the car."

I finally got back to the SUV. I quickly took the vitals of the one pinned under it and took out another orange piece of survey tape. On this one I wrote, "RES-OK, P-30+, 1521."

I reached for the kid who was moaning and took him by the shoulders. "Can you speak?"

He didn't answer, simply kept on moaning. "Can you hear me?" I asked again.

Still no answer. I took out another piece of orange tape and checked his vitals. Then I wrote, "RES-OK, P-29–, PERF 2–, 1522." As I finished, I looked up to see the teenager who had been holding a piece of bloody cloth earlier.

"Are you all right?" I asked.

She shook her head. "No."

"Can you tell me what's wrong?"

She said she'd been in the back of the SUV when it hit the other car. She remembered flying and hitting a tree. She pointed to the tree about 45 feet away. There was quite a bit of blood on the side of it. As she removed the cloth, I could see a small piece of branch protruding from the wound.

"What's your name?" I asked.

"Heidi."

I continued to talk to her while I did a quick assessment. She too would be an orange tape. After I had tied the tape to Heidi, I asked her who else had been in the SUV with her. She looked around and said she saw everyone but Carl.

"Carl? Was he walking around earlier?" I asked.

"Yeah, but he didn't answer when I talked to him. He just wandered off. Is he okay?"

I asked her to stay put and describe Carl to me. She did. I then called the battalion chief. "Command, Medical, I have six immediate, two delayed, and one unaccounted for. His name is Carl, five foot eight, 175, brown hair, yellow t-shirt. He was wandering when last seen."

Command acknowledged the information.

Medical Officer Duties

As I completed my triage, I changed focus. As medical officer, my job was to manage all the EMS resources. I left the immediate area and reported in to the battalion chief. He asked for my assessment. I told him that I had at least two parties who would need extrication from vehicles. As far as I could tell, we had at least nine patients. We would

Chapter 9: A Chance to Practice

need more ambulances for transportation to the hospitals and at least another engine company and rescue.

"Benjamin, here is what I have," he told me. "Right now, one engine and a rescue unit on scene. Another engine and rescue—ETA (estimated time of arrival) two minutes—and four ambulances from SAH (hospital). Think we can handle it with that?"

"Can we get at least two more ambulances?" I asked. "Since these are kids, I'd hate to see parents getting in the way. Let's get 'em treated and off the scene quickly before mom and dad get here."

"Good idea." With that, the battalion chief called for the extra units. While we were waiting for the additional ambulances, I established two separate working areas. The first was the proximity around the SUV. Engine 4 was in the process of getting the SUV off the patient, and Rescue 2's crew worked in tandem, providing patient support. Just as I was about to establish the additional work area, Engine 6 and Rescue 1 arrived. Command had instructed them to see me for their assignments after they had staged their apparatus.

I needed the crew from the engine to perform patient care and extrication on the patient in the car. So I assigned the working area to the engine company lieutenant.

Rescue 1 was given the duty of establishing a treatment area down the street from the accident site. This gave them approximately 30 feet of working area. Here they got oxygen on the patient, established IVs, checked for bleeding, and reviewed all the vitals, which would be needed before they got to the hospital. This took only a couple of minutes. We all knew more definitive care could be given in the hospital, not in the middle of the street.

Further down the way, I established a transportation area in a parking lot adjacent to the street. This is where the patients would be picked up for transport to the hospitals. The ambulances could come in one entrance and out another without getting in the way of the scene. I briefed Command on what I was doing, and he relayed the information to the communications center so the incoming ambulances would know where to pick up their patients.

Ladder 1 arrived on scene. I didn't know that Command had called for the crew, but I was sure happy to see them. These guys helped shuttle patients from the scene to the treatment area. I guess I'll never again assume "truckees" are good for only breaking and entering. They carried patients from where they were found on scene to Rescue 1's treatment area. From there, patients were loaded into waiting ambulances where their care would come from the paramedic on board.

With everything that was happening, before I realized it Carl had been found and transported to the hospital. All of our "immediate" patients had been taken from the scene to the hospital except for one—the driver of the car. They were still working with the jaws to get him out. That left one immediate and two delayed. I looked at my watch. It read "1538." Not too bad. 26 minutes from the call to now. But we still had three patients on scene.

I looked over to the ambulance staging area. My two delayed patients were receiving the finishing touches from Rescue 1 and were being packaged for transport. The last ambulance we would need was backing into position. As I watched, the ambulance company personnel closed the doors to their rigs and transported two more patients. The last one had just been taken to the treatment area.

As they placed that patient in the ambulance, I called Command. "Command, Medical. Last patient loaded. Request permission to demobilize treatment and transportation sectors."

"Command copies, permission granted."

I was tired. I hadn't figured on a two-car MVA to have nine patients. It was a resource-intensive call, and I thought all the crews had done outstanding jobs, so I walked over and told them what great work they had done. They all appreciated the fact that I had gone out of my way to give them a pat on the back. I even heard as they were walking away, "…Not very often someone says we did a great job—usually we get told we parked in the wrong place."

When I thought about it, what he said was true, and it did happen a lot. So I would put that comment in my memory bank as something we could look at in creating our culture of service. Up and down the

Chapter 9: A Chance to Practice

line. Thinking back, I *had* just used a little of what I'd learned today from Stormy.

The chief wrapped things up on our end in no time. He was ready to turn the scene over to the police officers, who had an arduous job ahead of them. First, to find out exactly what happened, then to make sure the driver in the wrong received a citation and whatever penalties the law required. It was not up to the police officers to pass judgment, but they had to have a good idea of what happened before they noted it in their final report. I knew these guys. They didn't want to impact anyone's life unnecessarily. But they had a difficult and sometimes thankless job. I was happy to be a firefighter/paramedic today.

Shortly after Chief O'Reilly got off the radio with Communications, he got into the vehicle.

"Boy, what a call. Haven't seen one like that in some time. You did a great job today. I know I put you in a position where you didn't get to do a lot of patient treatment. But you'll have to get used to it. You're a lieutenant now. You get to organize and someone else gets the patient care," he said.

"Thanks…I appreciate the confidence you had in me. Hey, Chief, can you give me any insight as to what I could do better next time?"

"Well, ya did a great job. Creative thinking. But what happened to the triage tags?"

"My mistake. I didn't grab any from the mass casualty bag before I began my scene size-up. I had the survey tape and pen from the hose test, and I didn't want to waste time coming back to the vehicle to grab the tags."

The chief rolled his eyes up at my comment. I should have taken the tags when I got out, but my mind was racing about everything I needed to do. I simply got caught up in the moment.

"Takes a big man to admit his mistake, but I gotta say, great thinking on your feet. Innovate, adapt, and overcome. Matter of fact, the crews appreciated your color coding. They understood it. It was a mess out there. You kept your cool and handled it well."

"Thanks." I knew I'd hear about my colored tape from the crews when I got back to the firehouse. They would tease me, and I really wouldn't be at all surprised to find survey tape on my locker, my car, or over my bed when I woke up in the morning.

It wasn't long before we arrived at the station. The chief was back to his standard routine, reporting to Communications, "Battalion 3 back in quarters."

CHAPTER TEN

CREATING LEADERS AND ACCOUNTABILITY

Where People Want to Work

The day had flown by quicker than I expected, and I was looking forward to a quiet night in the firehouse. I had lots to review and wanted to see what gaps I had so I could fill them in during my time off. As I walked into the day room, one of the guys said, "Here comes Super Medic. Hey LT, are you and the BC having dinner with us tonight?"

I nodded that we were, and he promptly yelled, "Set two more places for dinner. We have guests."

Gee, I never figured I was considered a guest. Does that mean I get out of doing dishes? "Thanks," is all I managed to say before the station officer came out of his office.

"Hey, Frank, got a minute?" he asked.

The station officer, Mike Collins, was a veteran lieutenant, having been with the department about 12 years. Standing six foot two and proportionately built, he stood out with his silvery hair and dark features. Funny thing, he was the same age as me, yet he had all this gray hair.

"Sure, how can I help?"

He waved me into his office and motioned to the chair squeezed in the corner. "You did a great job today. My guys really appreciated the compliments you gave them after the call. Keep it up."

That really made me feel good. One of my peers actually said I did something right. "Thanks. But that's not why you asked me to come in here, is it?"

"In a way, yes. I want to make sure you start out on the right foot. I hope you're taking advantage of the officer development program. I wish it had been in place when I was a new LT."

"Why? Do you think this program is better than what you went through?" I asked.

"Much better. I had to learn my job by trial and error. I didn't get a chance to ask how others had done things so as to avoid making painful mistakes. If I had the opportunity to do it over again, I would hope that the fire chief would be here and make us use that flywheel gizmo of his."

"What do you know about the Healthcare Flywheel?" I asked.

"A while ago, the fire chief and Chief Black came to some of us and asked if we would be interested in a new concept they wanted to try within the department. Use us as guinea pigs, you could say, to see how the Healthcare Flywheel worked and if implementation would make this THE place where we wanted to work. Some were talking of leaving for more pay over at our neighbor's next door, and the chief knew he couldn't compete with the salaries they were offering."

"Really?" I asked. "Better pay doesn't mean a better job—the chief sure picked a good time to suggest a new concept. How did everyone feel about the flywheel?"

"Well, at first we looked at it with a slightly jaded eye. You know, when something appears to be a good concept, but you wait to see if it's the 'idea of the week' type of thing that will quietly pass if you simply leave it alone? Well, the fire chief taught us that leadership is an action word. So we studied how the flywheel works and the benefits we could reap if we adopted the concept. We wanted to understand it so no one could say we didn't give it a fair chance. We discovered the chief was

Chapter 10: Creating Leaders and Accountability

right. By creating the kind of department people wanted to work for, we could compete against those offering better salaries."

"Great! Say, Mike, I have some questions about the flywheel, and I wanted to work on some of this tonight while we had some down time. Do you mind if I pick your brain a little?"

"Sure, I'd be glad to help."

"All right!" I exclaimed as I pulled the chair out of the corner a little closer to Lieutenant Collins' desk. "I was talking with Captain Storm this afternoon, and he was telling me about the principles. We got as far as building a culture around service. I really wanted to..."

He interrupted me. "The flywheel principles are used to keep it moving. Right? Do you have the list with you?"

I took out my copy with the handwritten notes taken at Captain Storm's office.

"Good." He read the entire list again. "These are called the Nine Principles* in the healthcare industry, and I think we should start using that term too. Okay?"

> ## Healthcare Flywheel
> Nine Principles/"Prescriptive To-Dos"
> 1. Commit to Excellence
> 2. Measure the Important Things
> 3. Build a Culture Around Service
> 4. Create and Develop Leaders
> 5. Focus on Employee Satisfaction
> 6. Build Individual Accountability
> 7. Align Behaviors with Goals and Values
> 8. Communicate at All Levels
> 9. Recognize and Reward Success

Leadership Investment

"Let's see. You covered the first three, so the next one would be 'Create and Develop Leaders.' Fine, let's start there. In order for our department to be the best and reach its goals, we have to have great leaders. But in order to *have* great leaders, the department has to invest something in them. It needs to develop, equip, and sustain its current and potential leadership," Mike said.

"Why do people leave one department for another?" he asked. "Is it always because of money, better pay? I know that's the situation we

Chapter 10: Creating Leaders and Accountability

believed we were facing a while back, but we learned something when we began to use the flywheel.

"We found out that people most often leave because of leadership—or the lack thereof, I should say. Salary is actually way down on the list. We thought we were going to lose our crew to more money, but that wasn't the situation at all.

"Let me ask you... What comes to mind when you think of the work you do?"

"The excitement, the camaraderie, the calls, the fun..." I was about to go on when Lieutenant Collins interrupted.

"Exactly. You didn't mention pay because you didn't take this job to get rich. You chose it because you wanted to make a difference, and something about the work intrigued you. People recognize you as a firefighter, and that gives you pride, and you're appreciated. Am I right?"

"Sure, but..." I said.

"The point I'm trying to make here is that people usually don't leave *just* for more money if first, they enjoy the job, and second, they have a great leader. So by developing our supervisors and making them great leaders, people won't want to leave. The key to high employee retention is good quality supervisors who are well trained. Do you see why we want to invest in creating and developing leaders?" he asked.

I could see it as plain as day. If the department developed its leaders, they would be more likely to succeed and inspire others through their leadership. People would be less inclined to leave simply for more money. On the other hand, if leaders did not receive training, they would struggle with their jobs and perhaps be challenged beyond their capacities.

The only way an organization can truly succeed in living the values it holds close is to develop the necessary leadership skills in those it promotes. If firefighters and paramedics are not equipped with the tools to do their jobs, then they may not be successful. The same holds true for leaders. They need the tools to flourish at their jobs—in this case, leading.

Lieutenant Collins continued, "I could go on about the importance of leadership, but there's a good book that handles it much more in depth than I can do here. It's called *Hardwiring Excellence*, by Quint Studer."

I'd heard about this book before. I made note of it and looked up.

"But we really need to move on if you want to finish your list before dinner," Lieutenant Collins said. "How long do you think you'll work for this organization? Wait—before you answer, think about this. A good paramedic is in high demand right now. People from across the state are offering signing bonuses and higher salaries to get people just like you to work for them. Right?"

I nodded.

"When was the last time a headhunter called you or someone you know?"

I had never received a call, nor expected one. Then I remembered Joe, my preceptor during paramedic clinicals. He had accepted a job last week to be a medic on a medical helicopter operation out West. "Well, a friend of mine took a new job last week."

"So why did he leave? Was it different work, a greater challenge, more money? What was the reason he left?" Mike asked.

I made a mental note to call Joe and ask him how things were working out. I could learn a lot by talking to someone who had just gone through being a sought-after commodity.

"I think it was the leaders he had," I answered. "He mentioned he wasn't being used for the skills he had developed. And he was always telling me that the bosses never listened to his ideas and never implemented some of the changes he felt were needed in the organization."

Lieutenant Collins smiled the wily smile of the coyote, like I had fallen into his trap. "Exactly! That brings me to the next point on your list—'Focus on Employee Satisfaction.'"

Chapter 10: Creating Leaders and Accountability

Concentrate on Employees

"How do you do this as a leader? First, you emphasize the positive that helps keep your flywheel moving. Make sure everyone understands what was achieved during the previous period—for you, that would be the last shift. For other staff, it might be the last week. Find out how well you're communicating—the areas where you're successful, and others that need attention.

"Ask how individuals feel about their contributions. Do this either in public or private, but make sure you celebrate people's wins in public. Share examples of people you know who are making a difference. Make it personal and make it positive. Remember, this isn't just about how people feel, but it's a large part.

"Find out if there's anything they need to be able to perform their jobs better. Equipment? Training? Whatever. But you need to be asking to find out the answers. People aren't going to come to you at first. You need to set the stage and help them feel engaged and successful in working with you. This will be difficult. Some people call it 'rounding for outcomes.' Whatever you call it, make sure it happens before someone expresses a desire to leave the organization."

Instantly I thought of Chief Black and the questions she asked as she made her rounds. *So this is where it came from!*

Renters Versus Owners

Lieutenant Collins continued, "There are hundreds of things you can do to encourage and support the Focus on Employee Satisfaction point, but I think we need to move on. Let's look at number six: 'Build Individual Accountability.' This one will give you the opportunity to see both sides of many issues. Traditionally, we have used the line '200 years of tradition unimpeded by progress.'"

With that, I laughed. "You know it. 'We've always done it this way.'"

"Jokes aside, so far we have identified lots of things leaders need to do to make the culture of the organization better for everyone. How about ownership? Let me ask you, when you stay in a hotel, do you clean up the room before you check out? Do you make the bed? Where do you leave the soiled towels?"

I paid for the room for the night, why should I clean it? I thought to myself. "I have to admit I don't do any of those things."

"Of course not. Because you were simply 'renting' a room for the night, there was no ownership involved. Now, if you were staying at a relative's home, you might take a little more care. They're family. But renters act and behave differently from owners.

"We wanted to create a culture within our organization where people are inspired and have a sense of ownership. We wanted to build an environment where individuals are fully accountable unto themselves, where they will say, 'We don't need close supervision; we can do our jobs exceedingly well because we're part owners.'"

A Peer Interview in Process

"Come with me," Lieutenant Collins said as he stood up. I followed him down the hallway, where he knocked on a closed door before opening it. Inside, six people who were grouped around a table greeted us.

"Hi, guys, how's it going?" Mike asked. He gestured towards me, saying, "Meet Frank Benjamin, about to be promoted to lieutenant. He's been picking my brain about the Healthcare Flywheel. I wanted to show him a part of it in action."

"Welcome, Frank," one of the group said, smiling at me. "I'm Tom Chavez. We're in the process of peer interviewing Tim Raub, potential new firefighter for the department."

"Peer interviewing?" I asked.

Lieutenant Collins explained, "When we hire a new member of our team, everyone participates—not just the fire chief or the officers—everyone. We call this 'peer interviewing.' It gives us an opportunity to find someone we know we can get along with. And we take ownership in that person's success because we were responsible for the hiring decision. Let's sit down and listen for a few minutes."

Tom asked Tim, "Have you ever had to resolve a conflict with a crew member? How did you resolve it?"

I listened as Tim answered, mentally applauding his response. He said that right away he took his grievance to the other person involved and asked if they could talk, one on one. He listened to what the other guy had to say and really tried to see his side of the situation. In the end, the two of them worked it out between themselves and were careful not to involve the rest of the team.

Next in line, another firefighter seated at the table asked Tim, "Do you see any obstacles to a long-term relationship with this department?"

"Yeah," Tim said, grinning. "Getting hired."

We all laughed. Then he went on to explain that he liked a feeling of stability and described the length of time he had been at his previous jobs.

When he was finished with his answer, Mike stood up and I followed. "We've got some work to do before dinner. Thanks for letting us sit in."

In the hallway, Mike said to me, "Well, what did you think?"

"Why weren't they asking him about his qualifications?" I responded.

"Because I, as his potential supervisor, prescreened him for qualifications. The group in there asks what we call behavioral-based questions, designed to find out how well he'll fit in with our department's work culture."

As we got seated again in Lieutenant Collins' office, he went on. "Remember, we were talking about accountability and the part ownership plays in that. Peer interviewing is one of the best ways to inspire these behaviors. Why? Because the whole crew is ultimately responsible for whether or not Tim is hired. And if he is, you'd better believe they'll take ownership of his success since they have a vested interest. And he will be accountable to them for having chosen him. He'll work hard to show them they made a good decision.

"There's one more thing this whole process does for the department," he continued. "When we have the right people in the right places, employee satisfaction increases."

And the flywheel spins, I thought to myself.

"Now that we've talked about setting up ownership in the department," Lieutenant Collins said, "I have a question for you. How do we improve our organization?"

I thought for a moment. But then the light bulb in my head came on. "How about asking employees what *they* think are good ideas for improvement?"

"Perfect," Lieutenant Collins responded. "As listed in the Nine Principles, this is called 'Harvesting Bright Ideas.' The ideas…"

Just then there was a knock on the door. "Hey, LT, food's getting cold, people want to eat," the voice announced.

"Well, I guess that's it. Can we continue this another time?" Lieutenant Collins asked.

"Sure! Thanks, this gives me a better idea of how the flywheel keeps its momentum." With that, I followed Lieutenant Collins out to the dayroom to the big family-style dinner.

How It All Fits Together

After dinner I took my notebook back to the bunk area to review my notes and make some sense of what I'd heard. I was beginning to see the implications of adopting an attitude of making a difference—the hub of the flywheel.

I had to remember the Nine Principles, especially if I was going to live them. I looked at the list again.

Healthcare Flywheel
Nine Principles/"Prescriptive To-Dos"

1. Commit to Excellence
2. Measure the Important Things
3. Build a Culture Around Service
4. Create and Develop Leaders
5. Focus on Employee Satisfaction
6. Build Individual Accountability
7. Align Behaviors with Goals and Values
8. Communicate at All Levels
9. Recognize and Reward Success

Nothing jumped out at me. I reread the list. Then I saw it: Excellence, Measure, Service, Leaders, Employee Satisfaction, Accountability, Behaviors, Communicate, Success. That was it! Perfect. I could relate an acronym to my job as a paramedic: EMS LESs ABCS.

Essentially, my job is to provide emergency medical service—EMS. As paramedics, our first priority is the minimum a person needs for life: airway, breathing, and circulation—ABCs. After the ABCs, we work to stabilize other possible causes of the patient's pain, injury, or illness. But those three are our first concern. We wouldn't be successful in providing emergency medical service without the ABCs. So, EMS minus—or LESs—the ABCs is easy to remember! The flywheel turns because EMS LESs ABCS.

TACTICAL CONSIDERATIONS

Create and Develop Leaders. You've heard it all before. It's common sense. Lieutenant Collins said it best. To paraphrase: In order for your organization to be great, you have to have great leaders. That means you have to invest in them. Your single greatest resource is your people. You need to develop, equip, and sustain current leaders and those you're looking to for continued success.

An organization cannot succeed in living its values (i.e., integrity, teamwork, and respect) and its organizational foundation pillars (quality, service, people, growth, and finance) unless it invests in developing leadership. There is a natural organizational evolution. Understanding the five distinct phases will help you determine what development needs are required at each step of the process.

1. Learn about the five phases of organizational change: The Honeymoon, Reality Sets In, Uncomfortable Gap, Consistency, Leading the Way—Results. In each of these phases, there are expectations and key action steps that must be considered in order for the organization to grow. More information about these phases can be obtained at the Studer Group® website at www.studergroup.com.

2. Moving organizational performance to the next level will require you to communicate to your team how they are performing. These conversations with your highmiddlelow®

performers will determine which direction you will take to success. I choose "conversation" instead of "counseling session" since you will have different discussions based upon where the team member is in your organization. High performers will need little encouragement, but you will need to re-recruit them periodically. Encouragement, development, and reward will be important. Middle performers will need encouragement, support, coaching, development, and reward. Low performers will need to understand why they are underperforming. Let them know the consequences of continued low performance, and show support by encouraging them to change. Low performers should not be considered people you want to keep until their performances have improved.

3. Leadership Development Institutes. Great organizations develop their leaders through formal educational/training sessions. For instance, in this book, Frank Benjamin is participating in a New Officer Orientation program. While this is just one example, your team can provide more.

Focus on Employee Satisfaction. In Chapter Four, we witnessed Chief Elle Black focusing on employee satisfaction through rounding. She asked these strategic questions: What is working well today? Are there people I should be recognizing today for their outstanding effort? Is there anything we can do better? Do you have the tools and equipment to do your job?

When you finish rounding, make sure you follow up. If you hear that Captain John Smith has done an outstanding job on this or that call, send him a note letting him know that you appreciate the effort he has taken. Be specific and let him know exactly what he did. The result? The behavior is likely to be repeated.

Again, common sense, but not common practice. Evidence has shown that employees want three things:

1. They want to believe the organization has the right purpose.

2. They want to know that their jobs are worthwhile.

3. They want to know that they make a difference.

Build Individual Accountability. The focus of building accountability is to create a sense of ownership. Employees come to understand that their behaviors, in line with the department's pre-set goals and objectives, control the organization's success or failure. Fostering ownership can begin with peer interviewing.

CHAPTER ELEVEN

NOT A FALSE ALARM

Smoke in the Hallways

I had been reviewing my notes for about an hour when the alarm tones when off. "I guess this is going to be a busy night," I mumbled to myself as I bounded down the stairs.

The entire firehouse was being sent to an "activated fire alarm." Usually these were what we considered "false alarms," but occasionally they weren't. Tonight the fire alarm was at SAH—the local hospital we had sent patients to earlier in the day.

Reminiscing about the hospital, I recalled it was first established in the early 1880s to take care of railroad construction workers. At that time, it had only 50 beds in a three-story building. Overlooking a lush, nature-inspired park, it was considered state-of-the-art. During ensuing years, the hospital had been added on to and remodeled many times. As new construction blended with old, the hospital continued to evolve.

Today, it's a sprawling complex covering approximately 50 acres, with 600 beds and 16,000 annual inpatient admissions. This is in addition to the 75,000-plus outpatient visits for such care as cardiovascular treatment, physical therapy, and more. The hospital represents a very large investment in our community as both an employer and as a healthcare provider.

My thoughts jumped to the present as we sped down the street. We could smell the smoke as I watched the fire engine turn down 9th Avenue just ahead of us. After we rounded the corner, I could see that everyone on board knew this would not be the routine activated fire alarm. There was an instant change in everyone's demeanor. Hands flew to make sure coats were closed, gloves were on, and air systems engaged. The fire engine stopped in front of a building just short of the main double entry doors. Above them, I could see the white strobe flash of the fire alarm.

Ladder 31 and Rescue 31 were right behind us. Willy Kerrigan took the high-rise pack and headed into the building. Joe Carroll and I followed, dragging the rest of the high-rise equipment with us. Boyce and Coyle (the rookie) were still on the sidewalk donning masks. As I approached the alarm panel, I could see the alarm read "5 East." This floor is the respiratory wing of the hospital. Not a good place for smoke and patients. I radioed Chief O'Reilly, who had taken Command and was outside in his vehicle poring over the building preplans.

"Command, be advised this alarm is coming from 5 East. Multiple sensors have activated, and the switchboard has received calls from the nurse's station that the hallway is charged with smoke and they are beginning evacuation," I said with as much calm as I could muster.

"Command copies—5 East, multiple reports of smoke in hallways. Staff has begun evac," repeated Chief O'Reilly. "Communications, this is Battalion 3. I have assumed 9th Avenue Command and I will need an additional alarm at this location."

As I returned to the battalion chief's vehicle, he grabbed me and pulled me closer. "Kid, I want you up there. You're to work with Lieutenant Collins on the fire floor. You'll be Division 5, and Lieutenant Collins will take fire attack."

I acknowledged his orders and packed up. Before I knew it, I was at the elevators ready to board. The backup team was there as well. I inserted the elevator key into the fire department operation slot and activated it. Once the crew was in the elevator car, I punched the

Chapter 11: Not A False Alarm

button for the fourth floor. *I hope this works,* I said to myself. This was the first time I'd been in a "real" fire situation where I needed to use the fire department operation feature of the elevator. Since we didn't want to have fire enter the car, we were going to the floor below the fire floor and taking the stairs the rest of the way. On the way up the stairs, the team attached their hose line to the fourth floor standpipe.

The Room on Fire

Lieutenant Collins was waiting for us on the fifth floor with his crew, crouched low by a door with smoke pouring out over his head. There were 12 rooms on this wing of the floor in a U-shaped pattern, with three of the doors open. Further down the hall, heavy black smoke was coming from under the door in the next to last room. On the other side of the hallway, staff were working hard to get their occupants out, and everyone seemed to be fleeing the area as best they could. Lieutenant Collins opened the door a little further, stopped for a moment, and then with his crew rushed into the hallway adjoining the room on fire. He started by forcing the door with all his strength. Smoke rushed through it, darkening the hallway and our vision.

Captain Murphy arrived with firefighter McCarthy behind him. "Give me a man with a Halligan," the captain yelled to me, and the two of them hustled to a room four doors down. "I'm sure I heard someone in there."

The captain and his team were on their knees as McCarthy worked. After furious hacking, the door to the next room still wasn't about to open. McCarthy pounded a hole in the wall to gain access and tried to squeeze through—a 16-inch space between the two-by-fours. He couldn't make it, not with his mask on. He turned to take the mask off, but before he could shed it, Captain Murphy entered through the hole. I grabbed McCarthy by the shoulder and yelled as loudly as I could to be heard over the commotion, "Don't take that mask off. Your life depends on it!"

The door still had not been opened, and Murphy knew that only luck or the help of God would keep the whole place from lighting up. He crawled on the floor toward the bed, swinging his arms before him as if swimming the breast stroke. His hand was stopped by the bulk of a body lying on the floor. It was a big frame, and Captain Murphy struggled to drag it towards the hole in the wall. The fire raging in the next room was spreading fast toward this room.

McCarthy was just crawling through the hole as the captain reached it with the body. "Here, Cap, here!" McCarthy yelled, but the smoke was so thick he missed the hole.

McCarthy grabbed the body under its arms and pulled.

While this was happening, Lieutenant Collins and his team were opening the door to the fire room. Searing heat hit them square in the face. Without protective gear, everyone would have been severely injured. Boyce and Coyle reached the door with their hose line and began spraying a stream into the room filled with the fire's sizzle. The water hit the ceiling and the sound became louder as falling ceiling tiles, wet and steaming, hissed on the wet floor.

The fire darkened quickly, and the smoke banked to the floor. "Give me some more line," Boyce yelled.

His order was relayed back through the hall by Lieutenant Collins' voice, "Give us more line on the one and three quarters."

The hose moved forward, Boyce and Coyle with it. Kerrigan moved up, breathing easily in his mask. He was going to relieve Boyce on the line, but he bumped into something in the middle of the room. Feeling around the floor to see what it was, his hands touched another body. "I got a victim here!" he yelled through the mouthpiece of the mask.

Coyle joined him quickly and they carried the body out.

Jimmy Boyce moved slowly and deliberately through the second and third rooms, Lieutenant Collins next to him all the while, saying, "You got it, Jimmy. You got it."

As the room darkened down completely, Collins raised his radio and relayed, "Command, Attack. We have made entry into fire room..." The rest of the transmission was inaudible.

Chapter 11: Not A False Alarm

"Attack, Command, repeat last transmission."

After several seconds, Command repeated his request. Still no response.

"Division 5, Command."

"Division 5, go ahead Command," I said. All I could think about was the last transmission as I waited for what seemed to be an eternity.

"Do you have eyes on Attack?" Chief O'Reilly said calmly.

"Negative," I answered.

"Get me a PAR for your division."

A PAR is a personnel accountability report. In this case, I knew I had a backup team of four and could see each of them. The ladder company with Captain Murphy had four. I could see three of them. I reached out and grabbed McCarthy. "Where's Murphy?" I said as loudly as I could.

"Inside."

I looked at the hole in the wall and could see the top of Murphy's helmet squeezing through, followed by his shoulders and chest.

A Casualty

"Take your victim out when you get your team together," I told McCarthy.

McCarthy crawled past us with the body in tow. It was a boy about 16 or 17 years old, a strapping black youth. But McCarthy was a powerful man and carried him easily. The boy was still breathing, but barely. McCarthy knew he had to get some oxygen into him if he was to live, and began mouth-to-mouth resuscitation as soon as they hit the stairwell.

"Command, Division 5—two teams accounted for. Backup and Search. Heading down hallway with Backup to locate Attack. Search team exiting building with victim."

"Command copies one team exiting, other team with Division 5 to find Attack."

Somehow in all the activity, Coyle and Kerrigan were able to get by the Backup team in the hallway without being seen. They took their victim to the stairs and exited the building right next to the sidewalk. They laid the second body on the sidewalk next to the boy McCarthy had carried out, who was now being resuscitated by paramedics. Coyle looked at the body before him. She was in her late fifties, with her clothes nothing but charred bits of material sticking to her skin. She was so badly burned the flesh on parts of her face had opened so it looked like there were pink patches woven into black skin.

Coyle turned away, vomiting as a female paramedic readied a mask to put over the woman's face. The paramedic tilted the woman's head back, cleared the airway, and fitted the face piece onto her burned face. She held the mouthpiece tightly with both hands to ensure a good seal because it wouldn't work if the oxygen escaped. Coyle placed one hand over the other on the woman's chest, and he pumped like a heart, 60 times a minute. "I don't know if this is going to work."

"We have to try," the paramedic responded.

And they did, without success, for what seemed to be an eternity.

"Attack, Division 5," I radioed. I thought I heard a slight crackle on the radio and then repeated my radio traffic. "Attack, Division 5."

"This is Attack, go ahead."

"We need a progress report and PAR," I said.

"Fire appears to be out. PAR of two. Team of two left several minutes ago with a victim," Collins stated.

"Understood, fire out, PAR two, with two exiting with victim. Command, Division 5."

"Command copied the last traffic. Searching perimeter for two firefighters with victim."

Fortunately, Lieutenant Collins' crew was able to make a good attack on the fire and suppress it quickly. But it was not good to have firefighters missing and not know their exact locations during a dangerous situation.

"Command, Division 5—please send up overhaul crews and crews to help hospital personnel with evacuation of remaining patients. I am taking the attack crew with me to find missing firefighters and complete the primary search. I will remain with them until they are eyes on outside."

"Command copies."

We continued our search—room by room. With the exception of the rooms immediately adjacent to the fire room, the hospital staff did an excellent job of removing patients or protecting them in place. It was hospital standard operating procedure not to place personnel or patients in any greater danger than necessary during an emergency. Patients across the hall were protected in place—only a stop gap measure—until additional personnel could get to the floor with the proper equipment to get them out.

As we searched rooms looking for the missing firefighters, we marked the doors to rooms we had already searched or which had patients and staff inside. When we found an occupied room, we radioed Command and a crew was sent to move the patient to a safer area. A ventilation team was sent up to clear the air and assist us in searching faster to make this rescue more effective.

Within minutes, the radio call we had desperately hoped for came through. "Two firefighters and victim located safe outside."

This was good news. All our people were accounted for without injury.

Midnight

Concurrent with all the other activities, Engine 3 had stretched a line to the floor above the fire to check for extension. It was a good fire stop—no extension into the next floor nor any damage noted on the floor below. One room was lost, but we stopped the fire there.

My crew and I exited the structure shortly after hearing everyone was accounted for. Lieutenant Collins joined us and we began to talk about the fire, as we do after each one.

"Did you notice that the whole place lit up?" he asked. "You could see there was a lot of heat built up in that room. Pretty intense fire. It's almost as if there was gasoline poured on everything. Probably a flash fire. It would have burned through the whole place if it hadn't been held in check by the sprinkler system."

As the fire investigators arrived, they questioned the chief, Captain Murphy, Lieutenant Collins, and me as to what we saw. Their job was like that of police detectives—they tried to identify what caused a fire. If it had been set—by whom and how. They were firefighters just like us, except they liked putting together puzzles more than fighting the fires. They had special talents in chemistry, forensics, fire behavior, and fire suppression. After about 30 minutes of talking with us, they entered the hospital and began the scene investigation.

The last of the fire crews exited the building after finishing the overhaul work. We picked up our hoses, repacked them onto the fire engine, and everyone headed back to the firehouse. It was near midnight, and dark as soot. I never realized how dark it really was at this time. But tonight seemed darker than other nights.

In the Kitchen

After a fire, everyone was usually too keyed up to sleep much. Besides, we had equipment to return to "ready" for the next call. Luckily, it didn't take long because the engineer had made sure almost everything was ready before we left the scene.

Usually, after a "good" fire, everyone ended up in the kitchen for a cup of coffee, glass of milk, or something else to eat or drink. Some came straight from the fire with smoke-stained faces; others grabbed a quick shower and then came to the kitchen. Everyone had their own ritual.

Chapter 11: Not A False Alarm

It was odd to think that just a few short hours ago, we were all gathered around the same table enjoying dinner. This was a tough fire. But we all came home, and I was happy none of my crew were injured or killed tonight. Still, we lost somebody.

Ordinarily about this time, somebody would say something funny about this or that, something like, "Hey, Benjamin, nice helmet hair," or we would kid each other to break the tension.

Tonight, no jokes were made. We sat around the table talking for about another hour. Just as many of us were getting ready to go to bed, one of the investigators stopped by.

"Hey guys, good stop. You really worked that one. Could have been a lot worse if you hadn't taken the quick actions you did."

Then Mike Collins spoke up. "Heard we lost one, though."

The investigator continued, "Yeah, but you saved one who surely would have died, and the one we lost we believe may have caused the fire."

We all looked around the table in stunned silence. Nobody wanted to be the first to speak.

"The lady who died was in the hospital because she had been a life-long smoker suffering from coronary obstructive pulmonary disease, COPD. Everyone on that floor is in respiratory therapy, which means high concentrations of oxygen. It penetrates everything, and I mean everything. Tables, curtains, bedding, clothes.

"Well, this lady needed a cigarette. Twice today, the nurses had to stop her from getting cigarettes. They don't know where she got the ones we found in the room. They said they had removed all her smoking materials two days before, but tonight she had gotten her hands on more from somewhere."

We all looked at each other again. "It was around 10 p.m. during rounds that one of the nurses visited her room. After checking on the patient and taking her vitals, the nurse was walking out the door when she heard a click, click, click. As she turned, she saw nothing but a ball of fire coming from the oxygen tent above the bed. She was smart enough to close the door and run to the fire alarm pull station. When she got back, the fire was so intense she couldn't re-enter the room. Remember, it's not the oxygen that burns; it's everything around it."

We talked with the investigator for another 30 minutes. He kept telling us what a great job we did and how lucky we were. This was a good team, and I was proud to have been on this fire with them. Slowly, each of us drifted back to the bunk room. Each in his own time.

The rest of the night was quiet. I didn't get much sleep. Since I was assigned to the battalion chief, I was afraid I would sleep through a call or not be ready when he needed something. It was a restless night.

At shift change, I was happy to see my relief arrive 30 minutes early. He came in knowing this was not my usual assignment and thought I might be tired. He didn't know how true that really was. Yet I wanted to stop by Admin on my way home and make another appointment to meet with Chief Black. Just as I got to the door of the firehouse, Chief O'Reilly stopped me.

"Hey kid, good job yesterday. You know, of course, not every day will be as exciting," he said with a smile and a wink.

"Sure, Chief, thanks again for all the help. Now comes the hard part—living up to those expectations."

"No problem, kid. Keep your head on straight and you'll do fine. Be safe out there." With that and a wave over his shoulder, he left the building.

CHAPTER TWELVE

RETAINING THE BEST

Leader Accountability

The next morning, I headed for the Admin building, hoping Chief Black would be there early again so I could talk with her. Things were beginning to fall into place and make sense to me, but I had more questions. And I needed to finish learning about the Nine Principles.

By the time I pulled into the parking lot, it was almost 7:00 a.m. Again, there were very few cars in the parking lot and the side door was unlocked. The door's mechanism hissed as it closed after I entered the building.

"Back here," a voice said. As before, I found Chief Black sitting at a table in the break room with a steaming cup of coffee in her hand.

"I had a feeling you'd show up this morning with more questions. The feedback I'm getting is that you are well on your way to understanding the Healthcare Flywheel. Can I get you some water or juice?"

She had a good memory in recalling I didn't drink coffee. "No thanks, just have a few questions. Nothing like last time," I said.

"Great! Let's go to my office."

I followed her down the hallway.

Once there, she said, "Have a seat. Where do you want to begin?"

I took out my copy of the Healthcare Flywheel and the principles, placing it on the table in front of me. "As I've been reviewing the flywheel concept, I've also been working to understand the Prescriptive To-Dos. During my interviews, I learned about the first five and how they help maintain the flywheel's momentum. Yesterday, I briefly touched on Build Individual Accountability with Lieutenant Collins, but I really want to hear what you have to say."

> ## Healthcare Flywheel
> ### Nine Principles/"Prescriptive To-Dos"
> 1. Commit to Excellence
> 2. Measure the Important Things
> 3. Build a Culture Around Service
> 4. Create and Develop Leaders
> 5. Focus on Employee Satisfaction
> 6. Build Individual Accountability
> 7. Align Behaviors with Goals and Values
> 8. Communicate at All Levels
> 9. Recognize and Reward Success

"Okay, let's see—building accountability. Employees are responsible for taking ownership of their behavior and making sure it benefits the organization. They're expected to act like owners versus renters. An owner cares and goes out of the way to excel and promote the good of the organization. Owners ask each other for advice and input instead of placing blame. They foster cooperation and teamwork, eventually finding common ground for action to accomplish goals."

"Okay," I said. *That's basically what we talked about.* "But what I am trying to understand is where I fit in with accountability as an officer."

The Behaviors

"That's a great question, Frank. First, let's talk about the behavior part—it's important to understand it because being accountable incorporates people's behaviors. Now, the behaviors we scrutinize are: Do people exhibit integrity in their dealings with the public and other employees? Are people competent in their jobs? Do they show flexibility in doing their work and how they respond to our customers? Are they able to make decisions based upon internal and external factors? What are their organizational skills? Do they have the ability to follow through with what they are working on? Are they dependable? And lastly, do they exhibit creativity in getting things accomplished?"

I watched as she wrote the desired behaviors on my Prescriptive To-Dos list.

> Competency
> Integrity
> Flexibility
> Decision-Making Ability
> Organizational Skills
> Ability to Follow Through
> Dependability
> Creativity

"These are the things we look for in each other, employee to employee, employee to supervisor, supervisor to employee, and so on. Up *and* down the chain of command.

"I heard you sat in on a peer interview yesterday," she said. "The team was asking behavioral-based questions, and these are the qualities they base their questions on."

Interesting, I thought. *So this is how the group comes up with what they'll ask.*

"But the peer interview process isn't foolproof," she continued. "Most of the time, we do a very good job of deciding on the right people to hire, but occasionally not. This is where you come in. When you see a person lacking, you're responsible for encouraging development of the skill and helping the employee. At the same time, you have to be careful—*you* might see a weakness, yet the employee might feel he has excellent skills in that area. So find out first if the individual agrees with your assessment, and then you'll know the approach to take."

"Thanks for the heads up," I said. I could see where this was a personal thing that had to be handled in a certain way so as not to offend.

The chief continued, "But once you've identified the limits an individual has, talked with the person, and pointed out the way to grow, then the employee becomes accountable for taking action to improve.

"And there is a flip side to this as well—sometimes it's all about the leader instead. Most employees want certain traits in their supervisor. They want a leader to be approachable and willing to work side-by-side with subordinates, doing the dirty work as well as seeing success. Employees want the supervisor to work with them to create efficient systems to improve the work they do. They want to get the training and development to do their jobs well and the tools and equipment to do the jobs right. They want to have a good relationship with their supervisor—not an adversarial one. But most of all, people want to be appreciated for the contributions they make to the team or the organization.

"That's also part of your job as a supervisor—you're accountable for all the behaviors I just described. If you don't meet the needs of employees, they will leave the organization for another."

"Lieutenant Collins brought up that same point yesterday, and it really surprised me. We talked about how people leave most often due to lack of leadership—it's usually not about salary," I interjected.

"He was right on," said Chief Black. "And when that happens, the department is out large sums of money due to its investment in employee training and benefits. It's far more cost-effective to find ways to retain employees by making the environment one where they want to work. Yet you need to understand that what the department needs is just as important. So there's a balance we work very hard at achieving every single day."

Bright Ideas

Chief Black continued, "One way we strive for that balance is a program developed to harvest intellectual capital—the 'Bright Ideas' campaign. When we launched it over two years ago, we could hear the groans coming from the firehouses. 'Here comes another one of those programs,' and, 'I guess I can wait out another program until they get another bright idea.'

"But the program lasted and has produced some great benefits, such as the 'brush coats' firefighters now wear on wildland fires. They were using a full set of heavy, bulky bunker gear. The cost of the coats was balanced against the number of lost work hours due to heat stress and other problems caused by not wearing the 'right' gear in the right environment. Another is the new officer orientation program. Right now we're not sure how this will pay off, but if what you are learning is any indication, it will be well worth it."

Those were great ideas. I had wondered where they had come from.

"What made Bright Ideas a success? We knew that in order to make it work for us, people had to believe their ideas mattered. That's why we set up a task force in the very beginning that was, and is, responsible for overall direction of the program. First, the team communicated what Bright Ideas was all about and asked employees to contribute suggestions that would help the department meet its goals or improve. Then they established a process for all divisions to review the Bright Ideas, which means the suggestions flow up to the senior leadership more quickly.

"Task force members also figure out how best to take advantage of a quality idea, or simply take an average one and make it better. And they train people on how to implement the suggestions.

Chapter 12: Retaining the Best

"Now for the best part—the task force recognizes employees for their ideas and innovations. Initially, when an idea is suggested, the employee receives a thank-you note. Next, if the idea is implemented, the employee is recognized with a reward based upon the individual's needs and those of the department. Finally, when a number of ideas have been implemented, the employee receives additional recognition.

"This is all the employee sees happening. However, behind the scenes, the task force monitors a tracking system to identify the impact of implemented ideas. Is the outcome a financial benefit? Does it improve our service? Tracking ideas and showing their effect proves to the fire chief that the program is feasible and worth continuing.

"The last part of the task force's duties is to work closely with the fire chief in continually redefining and focusing the goals so the program stays relevant. This department has proven that the Bright Ideas initiative is good for the organization, and I believe the fire chief will keep funding it to keep it around.

"What has it achieved for us? How we are perceived by the community has improved, for one thing. We've also kept rising costs in check. But perhaps most important, it's another way for employees to demonstrate ownership and to feel valued. When they contribute great ideas on how to streamline some practices or improve the quality of training, they become part-owners in the success of our organization. It also helps keep employees focused on the center of the flywheel—when they see they've made our organization better, they renew their Purpose, know they provide Worthwhile Work, and realize they are Making a Difference in the lives of everyone they touch.

"Frank, you said you wanted to know where you as a new officer fit in with accountability. Have I answered that?"

"Yes, and it's a lot more complicated than I thought it would be," I replied.

TACTICAL CONSIDERATIONS

Bright Ideas. Another avenue for tapping into the wealth of information your employees bring to the table is a Bright Ideas program. This initiative consists of a process developed to evaluate and track employees' ideas for improving the organization. In turn, employees are rewarded, which encourages even more ideas. You may be thinking, *Common sense.*

But again, it's not common practice.

Bright Ideas can make a huge difference in the organization's bottom line. But remember, the program's success hinges on how your new ideas are handled. Don't lose the enthusiasm of your team through negative talk and street humor. Actively work to improve the process.

1. Set clear goals and communicate.
2. Establish a process for evaluating the ideas.
3. Reward and recognize innovation.
4. Train your leaders on how to respond to innovative ideas.
5. Define the process for tracking and accountability.
6. Launch and celebrate ideas and focus on organizational goals.

30- and 90-Day Meetings. When a new employee is hired, meeting with that person after 30 and 90 days on the job is very important. It paves the way for good communication and good rapport with the employee. It will assist in establishing benchmarks and honest evaluation of the employee's skills and progress when first hired. While this subject is not covered in the story, it identifies problems that impact retention. For best results, ask the exact same questions of each employee:

- Is the job what you expected, and did we clearly communicate your responsibilities during the interview? Who has been helpful to you during the past 30 days?
- Do you have the tools and information you need to successfully perform your job? Is there anything you need from me?
- What ideas from your past experience might work here?
- Do you feel this is an organization that you look forward to being a part of and that we are meeting your needs?

Too often, emergency service organizations are a fluid group. People change from one organization to another. Since we hire people for their expertise, it's not unusual for them to say, "At ABC, we did such and such a certain way."

But what's the next thing you hear? Someone telling the new person, "I don't care how you did it at ABC. This isn't ABC, and this is how we do it here."

The 30-day meeting gives the new employee an open forum to express the pluses and minuses of your environment. That person can express ideas openly without fear of retribution or belittling. It presents a valuable opportunity to hear some great new ideas.

At the 90-day meeting, ask another question. "We realize having the right people is the key to an outstanding organization and a great place to work. Do you know of any candidates you would recommend to work here?"

CHAPTER THIRTEEN

ALIGNMENT, COMMUNICATION, AND RECOGNITION

Behaviors in Line with Goals and Values

"Are we ready to move on to the remainder of the Nine Principles, Frank?" the chief asked.

I nodded.

"Good. The next Prescriptive To-Do is 'Align Behaviors with Goals and Values.' So far, we've talked a lot about what to do for employees, but this principle directly affects our leaders. If we want to sustain what we have accomplished with previous Prescriptive To-Dos, leaders must be accountable for implementing objectives and meeting desired outcomes. They must be loyal to achieving results.

"Therefore, we've implemented a program to measure results. Its foundation is a leadership evaluation tool that holds all leaders accountable for actual outcomes rather than mere effort. By setting clear and objective goals, you create a roadmap to connect between actions and results.

"That makes this a better place to work, while our community receives better care. We have gotten the Healthcare Flywheel to spin continuously with little effort. But don't be fooled—there is effort. And that is why we have to hold our leaders accountable for goals and results of the organization.

"Leaders are actually evaluated based on how well they meet the organization's goals. They can see clearly how actions are connected to results, which helps keep the flywheel spinning."

Communicate, Communicate, Communicate

"The eighth principle is 'Communicate At All Levels.' If I want to get the message out about a new protocol, I have to be persistent. I need to repeat it numerous times and in various ways. Plus, I need to communicate to everyone, not just the officers, because it may not get passed along. Let me use an example. When I first took this job, the rumor mill worked pretty efficiently. At one point, I needed to tell the firefighters and paramedics about a new protocol just implemented statewide. I chose to go to each station, in person, to report the recent protocol. Yet the crews already knew what I was going to tell them courtesy of rumors. Was what they heard accurate? More to the point, can we consider rumors to be communication?"

"Well, yes, in a way they're communication," I answered hesitantly.

"But there is no accountability for whether or not the rumor is correct. Most of the time, as you well know, it contains only a bit of the truth that has been taken and twisted. A few days ago, you were the subject of a rumor that you were forcing your lieutenant out. Remember that?"

"Boy, do I!"

"So I continued to visit each station to ensure accurate information and details describing what the new protocols required was passed along. I visited every firehouse, presented the protocol to the officer, and in turn, the officer passed it along to his crew. I sat in as part of the audience, yet was available for any questions or clarification. I did this for every shift and every member of this department. And I followed up if there was a need for clarification. If I had simply passed the information off to a lieutenant or paramedic and had not been accountable for the communication aspect, what do you suppose might have happened?"

"There might have been mistakes, possibly life-threatening ones."

"You're getting the idea. It's not that I had to visit every single person to get the word out, but I wanted to prove to the rank and file how crucial accurate communication really is. By going house to house, they not only saw how important this protocol was to understand and implement, but they got the message that they needed to be accountable for how they communicate.

"I saw firsthand how important it was to let the officers communicate to their crew, and not appear to take them out of the loop. Obviously, having a chief officer visit every firehouse for every little thing is not effective. But they needed to learn about me, and I them. In a way, it developed respect between the leaders and me, and I saw the same between the leaders and the crews.

We learned the need to communicate at all levels—across the breadth and depth of the organization. If we find the communication is not effective or not being accomplished, today we simply find the bottleneck and come up with a solution."

The Power of Storytelling

"A few minutes ago, you mentioned communicating in various ways—such as?" I asked.

"There are some basic communication tools everyone has at their fingertips. One I think is particularly effective is storytelling. Never underestimate the power of storytelling."

"You mean like 'Once upon a time…'?" I said, laughing. As soon as it came out of my mouth I knew it wasn't what she had in mind.

"That's not exactly what I meant," she said with a serious look on her face. Then all of a sudden she also burst out laughing. "You are too much," she said. "Here I am pouring out all my years of hard work, book reading, studying, pushing, and pulling for information, and then you perk up when I mention storytelling. But that's what's so great about communication—there are so many ways to accomplish it, but some work better than others. Let me ask you, what do you remember better—the movies you have seen or the technical manuals you've read?"

"The movies, of course," I said matter-of-factly. That was a no-brainer. I didn't enjoy reading technical manuals, but I did like movies. It stood to reason I would remember more of what I enjoyed.

"Exactly. You remember more of something pleasant to you or something that challenges your psyche. Technical manuals, while challenging, don't always pique your interest. Let me use an example. A friend told me a story about two paramedics sent on a call to assist a lady who was having difficulty breathing. When they arrived, they determined she needed to go to the hospital. They packaged her up for transport and almost had her to the hospital when she realized she wasn't wearing her 'lucky slippers.' Her demeanor immediately changed to fear. Her hold on one of the paramedics was like a death grip. As soon as he realized this, he told her that he would radio the firefighters who had responded with them to see if they could pick up her slippers.

"Well, as things would have it, the engine company was on another call, so as soon as the paramedics could get away from the hospital, they went back to her home. They picked up the 'lucky slippers' and returned to the hospital. At the nurse's station, they found out that the lady was not doing well and was not expected to live through the day. For some reason, this didn't deter them in the slightest. They went to the patient's room and placed the slippers on her feet. The change in her vitals was almost immediate. News of this flew up and down the halls, and the doctors began to think of it as a miracle. The simple act of these paramedics changed the course of this woman's day and possibly her life."

Chapter 13: Alignment, Communication, and Recognition

I sat there stunned. I would remember what she just told me for some time to come. I had heard the words "making a difference" so many times in the past few days, but this story made it so much more meaningful to me. I knew now why the chief was such a champion of storytelling. I felt excited and energized.

"Storytelling is another way of communicating purpose and values. In turn, people are inspired and moved to action. But people don't keep moving that direction unless they can 'see' where they are going and visualize the end result. Why, even the president of the United States energized America to reach a goal by using storytelling. He made that goal the life's blood of his administration."

"The president? Which one?" I asked.

"John F. Kennedy. Do you remember his goal?"

"Of course, to put a man on the moon by the end of the decade!" I said, proud of myself for knowing my history.

"Right. It was in the early 1960s when he announced it was his administration's goal for America to be the first nation to go to the moon. But what held him back? Budget? Technology? Remember," she paused, "this was before the Internet and cellular telephones. As a matter of fact, it was before CDs, DVDs, or even videotape."

"I would guess technology?"

"Then explain why the United States was able to land a man on the moon in July, 1969," she said without hesitation.

"We were excited; we had a plan and a dream. We could do anything back then."

Chief Black gave me "that" look again. "So we can't do anything even remotely as big today?"

"I didn't say that," I said defensively.

"But you implied it. The Kennedy administration's NASA program overcame huge obstacles. They designed rocket systems, on-board computers, breathing air systems, communications systems, and so much more. All that inventive technology, by our standards today, was primitive. Yet we still made it to the moon by the end of the decade. How?"

"Because President Kennedy told us we would!"

"No, President Kennedy told us it would be difficult." Just then she got up. "Wait here," she told me.

After a few minutes she returned, handing me a piece of paper with President Kennedy's picture.

"Here, this is for you."

President Kennedy's
Special Message to the Congress on Urgent National Needs
May 25, 1961

If we are to win the battle that is now going on around the world between freedom and tyranny, the dramatic achievements in space which occurred in recent weeks should have made clear to us all, as did the Sputnik in 1957, the impact of this adventure on the minds of men everywhere, who are attempting to make a determination of which road they should take. ...We have examined where we are strong and where we are not. Now it is time to take longer strides—time for a great new American enterprise—time for this nation to take a clearly leading role in space achievement, which in many ways may hold the key to our future on Earth.

I believe we possess all the resources and talents necessary. But the facts of the matter are that we have never made the national decisions or marshaled the national resources required for such leadership. We have never specified long-range goals

Chapter 13: Alignment, Communication, and Recognition

on an urgent time schedule, or managed our resources and our time so as to insure their fulfillment. ...

...But this is not merely a race. Space is open to us now; and our eagerness to share its meaning is not governed by the efforts of others.

We go into space because whatever mankind must undertake, free men must fully share. ...

...First, I believe that this nation should commit itself to achieving the goal, before this decade is out, of landing a man on the Moon and returning him safely to the Earth. No single space project in this period will be more impressive to mankind, or more important for the long-range exploration of space; and none will be so difficult or expensive to accomplish.

...Explorations which are particularly important for one purpose which this nation will never overlook: the survival of the man who first makes this daring flight. But in a very real sense, it will not be one man going to the Moon—if we make this judgment affirmatively, it will be an entire nation. For all of us must work to put him there. ...

...This gives promise of some day providing a means for even more exciting and ambitious exploration of space, perhaps beyond the Moon, perhaps to the very end of the solar system itself. ...

...Let it be clear—and this is a judgment which the Members of the Congress must finally make—let it be clear that I am asking the Congress and the country to accept a firm commitment to a new course of action—a course which will last for many years and carry very heavy costs: ...If we are to go only halfway, or reduce our sights in the face of difficulty, in my judgment it would be better not to go at all. ...

...It is a most important decision that we must make as a nation. But all of you have lived through the last four years and have seen the significance of space and the adventures in space, and no one can predict with certainty what the ultimate meaning will be of mastery of space.

I believe we should go to the Moon. But I think every citizen of this country as well as the Members of the Congress should consider the matter carefully in making their judgment, to which we have given attention over many weeks and months, because it is a heavy burden, and there is no sense in agreeing or desiring that the United States take an affirmative position in outer space, unless we are prepared to do the work and bear the burdens to make it successful. If we are not, we should decide today and this year.

This decision demands a major national commitment of scientific and technical manpower, material and facilities, and the possibility of their diversion from other important activities where they are already thinly spread. It means a degree of dedication, organization and discipline which have not always characterized our research and development efforts. It means we cannot afford undue work stoppages, inflated costs of material or talent, wasteful interagency rivalries, or a high turnover of key personnel.

New objectives and new money cannot solve these problems. This could, in fact, aggravate them further—unless every scientist, every engineer, every serviceman, every technician, contractor, and civil servant gives his personal pledge that this nation will move forward, with the full speed of freedom, in the exciting adventure of space.

"President Kennedy told us it would be difficult," Chief Black repeated, "and we would have to put aside our differences. We had to make a 'major national commitment' to move ahead 'with the full speed of freedom, in the exciting adventure of space' to put a man on the moon by the end of the decade and return that man safely to earth.

Chapter 13: Alignment, Communication, and Recognition

He told a story. He made people visualize the hardship and the commitment necessary to accomplish this goal. He left nothing to chance, but everything to the imagination. You could see what he was saying… it was a powerful picture, which, of course, created a spectacular result.

"I don't think there is a person who was alive at the time who doesn't remember where he was and what he was doing when Neil Armstrong placed his left foot on the surface of the moon on July 20, 1969, and said, 'That's one small step for man, one giant leap for mankind.' People remember President Kennedy's challenge. Many don't remember, though, that he was taken long before we had a man set foot on the moon. Remember, President Kennedy was shot November 22, 1963, more than five years before the lunar landing. But the story was remembered long after he was gone. It painted such a fantastic picture that no one was able to forget it.

"Storytelling and visualization serve as a source of inspiration and energy. Can you think of a picture that inspires firefighters?" Chief Black asked.

"Sure, the one from Oklahoma City where the firefighter is holding the child after the bomb went off in front of the Murrah Federal Building," I replied.

Photograph by Charles Porter

"So you understand how important storytelling and visualization are to moving the organization from good to great," she said.

I could relate to what she was telling me. My mind wandered back to all the training I'd received and the stories I had heard. It was the pictures in my mind and the stories that inspired me. Now, as an officer, I needed to make sure I incorporated this imagery when I had something special to get across or had to get people moving in the same direction. Boy, Chief Black had really laid out the importance of being a good communicator.

She continued. "Now don't wait and use only the big inspirational stories. Use everyday events. Talking about what people did well energizes them—and talking about what they did not so well brings about improvement. Don't forget the stories of what people have said on calls for assistance. Bring out and read the thank-you letters that have ended up forgotten in employees' files. I could give you example after example of material for storytelling, but I think you get the idea."

I did get the idea. Not just for the big things, but the daily motivators as well. To live life daily and not to wait for the big things—it might be too late.

I glanced at my watch. The office would be buzzing with activity shortly, and I had a lot of things to do today. I asked Chief Black if I could set up another appointment for the next day.

Looking at her calendar, she said, "I'm afraid I've got a busy week ahead. You have your promotion ceremony coming up. How about we get together that day, same time as this morning?"

"Okay, great." With that I excused myself and left the room. I was supposed to have lunch with Pete and Maggie and didn't want to miss hearing what they had discovered from their interviews.

TACTICAL CONSIDERATIONS

Align Behaviors with Goals and Values. In order to sustain the success an organization has achieved, a process must be established to ensure continuance of the desired behaviors and outcomes. This will require that a leader evaluation tool be implemented, its purpose being to measure how well that person achieved the organization's goals and objectives. However, you will need to be prepared to do one of two things: either reward leaders based upon those results and their demonstrated commitment to the organization, OR be willing to de-select those who're failing to achieve the goals. However, before de-selecting an individual, determine if the goals were clearly established, attainable, and measurable—important pieces of accountability.

When establishing an evaluation process, remember to ask yourself:

1. What are our top priorities? Are they appropriate to our mission? Are they important to managing our organization, people, facilities, and so on?

2. How do we weight them? Do we weight that the truck is in service mechanically for a frontline supervisor, or do we measure on-time performance for reports, emergency responses, and things within a supervisor's control?

3. Which things should we stop doing or do less of? Another thing to consider: If we're working with outdated technology or processes, can we really measure a leader's effectiveness based upon what is available to that person?

4. What do we do with leaders who're not hitting their targets? This will require soul searching on the part of the supervisor. If you are going to have consequences, you need to enforce them. Remember a line that Quint Studer uses in his presentations: "What you permit, you promote." If you condone leaders who are not meeting their goals, others will see their behavior as acceptable. If you do not enforce the process with everyone, there will be someone who realizes this and consequently may not follow you when you need that person most, or employees will figure it is okay to have a double standard.

Communicate at ALL Levels. When everybody understands what is important and what is expected, great things can happen. Leaders appear more effective, and employees feel empowered and willing to work for their own development. There are lots of ways to make this happen. They include:

1. Managing up—Eliminate the We/They discussion. No longer is it, "This came from Admin, so we have to do it." It now becomes, "Let me help you understand why and how this is important to our success." You can also manage up other units, people, and teams.

2. Employee forums—Allow for a direct exchange of information. But remember, if something is agreed upon in that setting, it is important to take action on it. This tool allows for a variety of opinions to be expressed, not necessarily in the vertical chain of command.

3. Communication boards—Be aware that more and more, the boards are being posted on secure electronic

systems for use within the organization. This system could be managed by a communications team whose members are interchanged on a regular basis. The end result is a continuous creative flow and constant learning on the parts of the team members.

4. Storytelling—A powerful and memorable tool. Its relevancy to your audience can be maximized by using a format to which people can relate, as well as recognizable, appropriate references.

CHAPTER FOURTEEN

COUNTDOWN TO CELEBRATION

Lunch with Maggie and Pete

It was rare that Maggie, Pete, and I did anything together, so I guess this was sort of a special occasion. We met at the local Irish pub, which was a restaurant and microbrewery. The building itself was a firehouse long ago—no kidding! It was decked out to resemble an old Irish pub with stained glass from the old country, casks, and pictures of Notre Dame's Fighting Irish gracing every spare inch of the walls, ceilings, and doors. It was a local hangout and a well-known spot for tourists to visit when they came to town.

Maggie and Pete had gotten there before me and were already seated at a table. I quickly sat down across from them and they stopped talking long enough to blurt out, "What took you so long? Get lost?" almost in stereo.

I got the same feeling I had before at the new officer orientation that these two were either brother and sister or married. And still neither was correct. Just then, our server arrived and took our orders. It was a good thing that I'd been here frequently and knew what I wanted to order, or else I'd have held everyone up. The place was bustling and I could tell the server was in a hurry.

"So," said Maggie, "what do you think?"

"About what?" I said.

"You know, this orientation stuff. Seems like a lot of hoops to go through just to get a badge and radio."

Not wanting to put my foot in my mouth, I opted for input. "You caught me cold. What do *you* think?"

Pete was the first to speak. "I think it's great. Yet, it seems like we have to do more and more to get promoted when we've already done enough. But the orientation stuff I think is really good. I learned some neat things from the people I interviewed. Makes me want to be a lieutenant right now."

"It was stupid," Maggie contributed. "I could have read about everything I heard during the interviews. It was a complete waste of my time."

Pete interrupted her. "Just because it's new and other people never had to do this doesn't mean it was a waste of time. Sometimes you just have to go with the flow, Maggie!"

"Humpf," came from Maggie as she crossed her arms and leaned forward on the table. "Go with the flow," she grumbled.

"You know," I chimed in, "going with the flow isn't always a bad idea." I felt like I was trying to be a mediator.

"I have worked hard to get here. Nobody is going to take that away. Not you, not him," Maggie said, pointing at Pete. "Not anybody. I am tired of all the hoops we have to jump through. Why does it change when a woman gets promoted?"

"Hey, Maggie, chill out," said Pete. "It's nothing personal. We're all doing it. If you were the only one, yeah, I could see why you might feel picked on. But Frank and I had to do everything you've done."

"Okay, okay. But still, how come we have to do all this stuff when it's never been done here before?" she asked.

"From what I've seen, the chiefs want to make this place better than when they took over," I replied.

"How ya figure?" asked Pete.

"Look at what was given to us, and what we were asked to do. Doors were opened to meet people we probably would never get to talk to unless we were in trouble or answering questions about some

Chapter 14: Countdown to Celebration

investigation. Right?" Heads nodded. "We were asked to do a little homework and given time to do it. They paid us to do our homework. Doesn't that show you that *they* are committed to our success?

"Let me ask you, Maggie," I continued, "do you remember the last people promoted and what you thought about them when they first started working at your firehouse?"

"Sure, I looked at them like some sort of rookie with more pay and more authority than I had. They had to prove themselves to me. I knew they didn't have a clue," Maggie said pointedly.

"Do you want that to happen to you?" I asked.

"Not really, I guess I didn't think about it from that perspective." The hostility seemed to drain from her body.

"Ya gotta go with the flow sometimes," I said again. "There are hidden treasures. Water is one of the most powerful substances on earth. When you hold it in your hand, it's soft and weak. Yet, when you're on the beach and a rip current pulls you under—you cannot survive unless you go with the flow for a while and swim parallel to the shore until you're out of the riptide. The chiefs are letting us hold the tools we need in our hands—watching us try to manipulate the 'water,' knowing full well we can't. But we're almost on shore. Once we are promoted, they are hoping we have learned enough so that if we are caught in the rip current, our training will allow us to survive and be stronger swimmers because of it. Does that make any sense?"

I thought, *Where did all that come from? Frank Benjamin, newly promoted lieutenant and philosopher!*

Maggie just shook her head with a smile from ear to ear. "Boy, I thought you guys were just my friends. Now I find out you're Socrates and Zeno of Elea."

"Who?" we asked simultaneously.

"What—you don't think I know anything about anything except firefighting? You both have got a lot to learn. Socrates was an ancient Greek philosopher best known for his work on dialectic, the idea that truth needs to be pursued by modifying one's position through questioning and conflict with opposing ideas. It's the idea of the truth being pursued, rather than discovered. Zeno of Elea was an Italian philosopher known for his puzzles and paradoxes about motion and plurality in the days before the development of 'logic.' He was around before Socrates."

"Where did that come from?" I asked.

"You started it with the water analogy. But you're right. I need to give all this orientation stuff a fair chance."

Just then the server delivered our meals. The rest of lunch was pretty much small talk. As soon as Maggie finished her meal, she stood up and announced, "Thanks for lunch, guys. You gave me some new ideas that I need to work through. Mind if I run?"

Pete and I looked at each other and shook our heads. "No."

She was off in a flash. In a second it dawned on us—we'd completely forgotten to ask her to pay for her meal. Pete and I simply stared at each other, not sure if we had been duped. Laughing, we paid Maggie's tab and commented that it was worth the education she had given us.

Call to Sandy

"Hi, Sandy, this is Frank Benjamin. Listen, so far I've been given information about eight of the Nine Principles®. Could you help me out with the last one?"

"Sure, Frank, let's see. Give me a second." I heard a drawer open and close on the other end of the telephone line, followed by papers rustling, and it sounded like the receiver had been hit with a sledgehammer. Then, "Sorry about that, I've been working on the department's NFIRS analysis and I dropped the phone. My apologies if I blasted out your ears.

"Let me make sure of what you've covered to this point. Stop me if you're not familiar with any of the principles I'm about to list. Commit to Excellence, Measure the Important Things, Build a Culture Around Service, Create and Develop Leaders, Focus on Employee Satisfaction, Build Individual Accountability, Align Behaviors with Goals and Values, and Communicate at All Levels. Okay so far?"

Chapter 14: Countdown to Celebration

"More or less." *I need something—some kind of cheat sheet—to help me remember these Nine Principles. Each item is so important, and together they embrace the whole concept.*

"All righty, then. I hope you don't mind, but I figured if I used more active words it would help you understand that the Prescriptive To-Dos are not effective unless they're acted upon. You just can't sit back and wait for them to happen. You need to take an active part."

"Thanks for the reminder." I knew she had a lot more knowledge about this subject than anyone, but why couldn't she just answer my question?

"Oh, it's so simple. You're going to kick yourself when you hear it. You ready?"

It was hard to be so enthusiastic after being up most of the night, meeting with Chief Black, and then eating lunch with Pete and Maggie. But I wound up my attitude and said, "Sure, I'm ready."

"The last one is Recognize and Reward Success. Although this is one important topic, it's easy to see how it can be forgotten. We all hope someone will recognize our efforts to be the best. Not always so. Yet if we get in the habit of recognizing success and rewarding it, then the behavior that brought it about in all probability will be repeated."

Recognize and Reward Success—I didn't think our organization was very good at this. Sure, we celebrated the great "save" when dealing with lifesaving measures, but that was part of the job. How about the guys who went out of their ways to help someone—they didn't get recognized nearly often enough. Now that I thought back, since I started this orientation process, I actually had begun to compliment people. I never did in the past. Why not?

"Frank, are you still there?" Sandy asked. I was so caught up in my thoughts that I almost forgot I was on the phone.

"Oh, sorry. Just thinking about what you said," I replied.

"This is probably one of the most difficult, in my book!" she continued. "Do it too much, and people think you're insincere. Too little, and they think you don't care. But I think it all boils down to sincerity and heartfelt thanks. How many times do you hear someone criticize another person? Often, I bet. I've heard it said that it takes three compliments for every criticism to create a positive work environment. So even if you have one for one, it still creates a negative work environment."

"That'll never work with firefighters. Too many compliments and their heads will swell up and pop," I commented jokingly.

"Have you ever seen a head swell up and pop from compliments, Frank?"

I wanted to swallow my words. I should know by now that if I want to be successful, I have to learn to keep my big mouth shut and not say the first flippant remark that comes to mind. "Sorry, I was just joking."

"That's okay. But it won't be okay to the person whom you are recognizing. If they think you are making a glib remark, they won't trust your compliments or your ability to lead at some point. Yet, I'm not saying a little lightheartedness isn't appropriate. Just watch when you use it. There will be a time and place, of that I can assure you. Besides, I can think of a few…"

"I'm sorry, it wasn't meant as it sounded," I said. "Can we start over?" *She could think of a few. Sandy really is cool*, I thought to myself.

With that, I began the conversation again. Before long, I had Sandy laughing with me, and we were able to work through my thoughtlessness at the beginning of our conversation. Sandy went on to explain to me that reward and recognition raise the bar on the behaviors we demonstrate every day. She emphasized how important it is to do these things on a regular basis, not just every once in a while. We need to be continually cognizant of everyone's accomplishments and acknowledge them for being successful. This reinforces positive behaviors.

"Frank, if you really want some good information on Recognition and Reward, you need to stop in here on one of your days off. There's a whole committee dedicated to identifying outstanding work and distributing appropriate recognition and rewards in our department. You ought to see all the different things the group does—way more than just presenting awards. It's a committee that really puts its heart into what it does. Did you ever receive a thank-you note for doing something outstanding?"

Chapter 14: Countdown to Celebration

"Yes, I got one for an outstanding public education presentation and another from the fire chief thanking me for my service to the department."

"That was partly the work of the committee. They make recommendations and provide the fire chief with the pertinent and vital information he needs in order to recognize a person or team. Then the chief writes and sends out the note under his signature. Great plan. How did you feel when you got it?"

"Wonderful. I really didn't know anyone was watching. I was just trying to help the public understand how the 911 system worked."

"That's the point. You didn't expect it, but I'm sure you'll take advantage of other opportunities that come along."

"Sure," I said. "I liked being recognized!" Then it hit me. Even though I thought of myself as an average individual, I felt on top of the world from something as simple as a thank-you note sent to my home. As a matter of fact, I showed it to Lexi, who made an even bigger deal out of it.

"You don't need to worry about whom you give recognition to, Frank. The more you give, the more results you create. In turn, that keeps the flywheel spinning and people aligned with the department's goals and culture."

"Thanks, Sandy, you've been a great help. Again, I apologize for getting off on the wrong foot today."

"Frank, I believe you will be a great officer and a gentleman. Good luck. If there is anything I can do to assist, please call me."

"Thanks again." And with that, I hung up the phone.

Sharing with Lexi

Once again home, I was looking forward to talking with Lexi at the end of her work day. I couldn't wait to tell her all that had happened and what I'd learned. But right now I had a little time to reflect on what I'd written in my notebook and to think about the influence I was expected to have as a new officer.

But first I had to play with the dogs for awhile to relieve some stress. As we romped mindlessly in the yard, something occurred to me. I had been too involved in trying to understand the Healthcare Flywheel to consider its far-reaching implications. Now it dawned on me that the flywheel was just *the analogy* I needed to reach beyond my current skills and abilities. It would help me get beyond my self-imposed limitations. It was the key! So simple, but it could be replicated by employees in any organization who needed to focus on excellence.

Time sped by and it was late afternoon before I realized it. I had relived the conversations with Chief Black, the telephone call with Sandy, as well as the rest of the events of yesterday. No wonder I felt drained—all that had happened in a little over 24 hours? I looked at my notebook one more time. In it, I had written, "Healthcare Flywheel—Purpose, Worthwhile Work, and Making a Difference." Then below I listed the Prescriptive To-Dos.

Chapter 14: Countdown to Celebration

> # Healthcare Flywheel
> ## Nine Principles/"Prescriptive To-Dos"
> 1. Commit to Excellence
> 2. Measure the Important Things
> 3. Build a Culture Around Service
> 4. Create and Develop Leaders
> 5. Focus on Employee Satisfaction
> 6. Build Individual Accountability
> 7. Align Behaviors with Goals and Values
> 8. Communicate at All Levels
> 9. Recognize and Reward Success
>
> *Prescriptive To-Dos List—Works hand in hand with Passion and Results to make the wheel turn*

While I was reviewing the stuff from yesterday, I also thought about the communication style we use in the firehouses. We joke A LOT. It helps lessen the magnitude of the tragedy we see. We laugh, tease, and banter back and forth, and it really seems to work for us. In becoming an officer, I'll really have to watch myself—think before I speak. I sure hope I can find a balance.

When I share what I learned yesterday with Lexi, I hope she won't find it boring. I was excited about the prospect of becoming the best officer the department ever had. If that sounded egotistical, it wasn't. But then, there had to be some ego involved for a person to want to be the best—or was that pride, drive, and determination? I didn't know—either way I was filled with enthusiasm about the things I'd discovered. It was more than I had expected, and I still seemed to have more questions than answers.

I heard Lexi's car enter the garage and the door begin to roll down. I walked to the kitchen entrance to greet her.

"Hey…how was your day?" I asked.

"Long day, but I think it was okay!" She set her notebook and bag down.

"Great, I ordered pizza if you're hungry. I spent the day reviewing my notes from yesterday and lost track of time."

"Pizza's fine. Let me change and freshen up. Give me five minutes," she said, kicking off her shoes. She took the stairs two at a time.

I set the table, and after the pizza arrived, we sat down and enjoyed a leisurely meal. We talked about her day and I skimmed over mine. After the plates were cleared, Lexi and I moved into the family room. We made ourselves comfortable and I began to tell her about yesterday's journey. As I talked, she appeared intrigued.

"Were every one of the new officers assigned the same tasks?" she asked.

"I don't know. I just interviewed the ones on my list and a few others because they had information I needed."

"Boy, if the fire chief knew you were going to be doing all of this research, don't you think he would have given you more time?"

After I thought about it, she was right. But I wasn't sure if more time would have made it easier or just prolonged what it took to get to the "finish line." I would have to ask the others how they felt.

We continued to talk about what I had learned throughout the past few days. After about an hour, Lexi held up her hand. "Enough already, my brain is full and beginning to hurt. Sounds kind of like pride and ownership. If you have pride in your organization and abilities, you will take ownership of them."

"Yes, but…" was all I managed to get out before she continued.

"No, not 'yes, but.' It's a culmination of trial and error. Those who developed this program had to go through some tough times—yet the benefit is if people take the Healthcare Flywheel as a tool to improve how they do their jobs, run their organizations, and so on, everyone will want to come to work and have a part in making a difference in a lot of people's lives—not just their own."

Chapter 14: Countdown to Celebration

That's it! The flywheel and its principles are more than simply a healthcare tool. It's a strategy that boils down to basic customer service. Both inside and outside the organization, customers are affected. "Inside" refers to staff, vendors, and others, while "outside" customers are clients, patients, their families, the community, and more.

Though Lexi had a different slant on what I'd been learning, she was as excited as I was.

She continued. "This Healthcare Flywheel—it incorporates many of the good administrative models we've seen in management classes. Doesn't it?"

I nodded.

It Takes Courage

"Let's see, goal orientation is addressed—mapping your destination, mentoring—helping others gain insight. 'Serving' leaders who benefit all levels of the organization, not just their own. It touches on reward and recognition, a culture of excellence, and goal measurement. I think the only thing that this flywheel thingy doesn't address is courage."

"Courage?"

"Remember when I told you how important courage is to be a successful leader? Remember when we read through those management books and said, 'All this is all well and good. But if nobody has the courage to follow up or follow through, then it's all for nothing'?"

"I remember," I said. "But the flywheel incorporates many actions needed for the wheel to turn in the first place. Doesn't it take a little courage to adopt such a tool, incorporate it into the business plan, train people on its use, and then monitor the results?"

"Sure, but why isn't courage specifically addressed?"

"I think it is. Here, let me show you…" This was indeed strange. I was a student for the last several days; now I was the teacher. "As a firefighter, I have courage to go into a burning building to try to rescue someone who is trapped or injured. Right?"

"Okay, I can see that firefighters have lots of courage, but what does…"

"Now look at it this way. Going into a burning building is courageous, as you readily admit. That's an action. Now, which is harder: working with someone to improve his or her skills or running into the burning building?"

"Depends. You have to be crazy to run into a burning building while others are running out," she said, laughing. "But I think you're right. I don't like to counsel employees for behavior issues or for not meeting goals or deadlines. I hadn't looked at it that way before. I guess you *are* right: People have to have courage in order to work on such a program. If they don't succeed, they face the consequences of a poorly received or managed organization. The backlash could be terrible. But on the other hand, it could improve the organization immensely. I guess the courage component *is* in this model."

I explained, "I think what I am trying to show you is that the *action* of getting the flywheel turning to provide the three distinct benefits—Purpose, Worthwhile Work, and Making a Difference—is the courageous component. But it's also integral to the entire movement of the flywheel, not something separate."

"You're right," Lexi acknowledged. "The Healthcare Flywheel touches on so many things that people involved in others' well-being must do in order for the organization to be great. I guess I just needed you to point out it takes courage to make the changes that go along with adopting the flywheel and making it spin."

With that, we called it a night and went to bed.

TACTICAL CONSIDERATIONS

Recognize and Reward Success. It has been said that everyone wants to feel special. When people feel valued for their talents and skills, their level of commitment soars. And for good reason. When you praise versus criticize, thereby calling attention to positive behavior, the behavior tends to be repeated. However, research tells us that there is a ratio involved here. Studies show that if you hand out three compliments and one negative comment, the person on the receiving end has a positive feeling and will repeat the praised behavior. If you give two compliments and one negative comment, the recipient is neutral to the events. And if you compliment only once and make a negative comment once, that person is not motivated enough to do the praised behavior again.

How many times have you heard, "It's all about the J-O-B"? Did you take that as a resounding recommendation of what the person was tasked with doing? No, most likely the comment was made by someone who simply shows up to receive a paycheck. Do you want to work or volunteer for this organization?

We have been trained to accept praise. As a child, when you took your first step, you received an enormous amount of praise. But today, when you walk into a meeting, people are pleased you are there, but they don't fawn over your ability to walk into the room. Just like "baby steps," growing reward and recognition beyond the basics takes time. The Disney organization has harnessed the need to recognize just how important every position is—regardless of the level. For instance, let's go to the lowest positions of customer service at a resort. Consider the towel boy. If there are not enough towels, the guests have a poor experience and may not return. This has a direct impact on the company's bottom line. But who was really responsible for the lapse in service? Was it the towel boy who was charged with fetching the towel with which you were to dry off? Or was it the stock clerk whose job it was to ensure that enough towels were on hand for the guests? Maybe it was the packaging person who failed to pack enough towels to fill the stock clerk's order? Or perhaps it was the individual who launders the towels? And let's not forget the delivery person who brought the clean towels to the resort. Every single person in this chain of lower level jobs is important to the success of the resort. If one link in this chain fails, the guest has a bad experience.

The same is true for the emergency services. If one link fails, the recipient of our services has a bad experience. And recipients are having bad days to begin with!

So how do we set ourselves up to raise the bar on the service we deliver and be the outstanding organization we want to be? One proven way is recognizing and rewarding the behaviors that lead to our success. To make this happen, here are a few tactics to consider:

- **Create a reward and recognition team.** When peers recognize each other's successes, it makes those successes even more special. Baptist Hospital in Pensacola, Florida, utilizes a WOW card developed by the team. The cards are distributed to employees for them to hand out as they see fit. When an employee sees a coworker delivering a WOW behavior, that person is gifted with one of the cards. It has space for the employee to fill out the coworker's name, department, date, and what they did to wow the customer. WOW cards are redeemable for a wide range of tangible rewards.

- **Write and send employee thank-you notes.** Don't underestimate the power of these—employees have been known to have the notes framed and mounted in a prominent place in their homes. When an employee is outstanding, send him or her a note—to that person's home. Not only do employees feel special, their families can enjoy the moment as well.

- **Reward and recognize all employees.** And don't forget the management team, who needs a boost as well. Remember to include support staff, mechanics, the Board of Directors, the City Council, and others. You get the idea. The more you reach out, the more you get back. Use this positive tool to create the organizational excellence you want in your team.

CHAPTER FIFTEEN

NEW OFFICER ORIENTATION WINDS DOWN

Last-Minute Jitters

I met with Chief Black at length early in the morning on the day of the ceremony. We talked some more about how employee outcomes could be managed through 30- and 90-day progress monitors. And she explained how to eliminate the we/they phenomenon and to manage up and down in the organization. She shared charts, tables, and reports on how organizations like major hospitals had adopted the principles outlined in the Healthcare Flywheel. During our discussion, I grasped how important it was to institutionalize *excellence*. Today, I actually felt like I was prepared for the next step in my career.

As the day wore on and 3:00 p.m. neared, I began to feel butterflies in my stomach. Perhaps I should have had that bagel earlier. I walked to the boardroom. Again, the table was set up pretty much as it had been for our first meeting with nametags placed in front of the seats we were to occupy. However, there was one distinct difference. Missing were the colored folders we were given last time. There was only a plain manila envelope in each place with our names and the date typed on a sticker in the upper right corner.

Since I was a few minutes early, I decided to go visit Chief Black one more time to see if there was anything else she felt I needed to know. As usual, Sandy was at her desk outside the chief's office.

"Hi, Sandy, how are you today?" I asked.

Sandy looked up, smiled, and said, "Hi, Frank—fine, thank you. Hope everything is going well with your 'little' project."

I chuckled. My "little" project had been to discover what made the Healthcare Flywheel turn. "I think I have a better handle on it. I hope I can do as well as everyone expects."

"Well, you know you have allies here. Just pick up the phone... besides, if everyone took half the interest you did in discovering the secrets of the Healthcare Flywheel..."

With that, her telephone rang. She answered it politely. Speaking to the caller, she said, "Elle, he's standing right here. Do you want to talk to him? Okay. I'll put him on."

Chief Black was on the other end of the telephone. Caught in a meeting, she was calling to wish me luck this afternoon. She didn't want me to feel that all the hard work I'd put into this process wasn't appreciated. She hung up quickly because she had to return to the meeting.

As the line went dead, I felt like a part of what I had worked so hard for since the first day had just evaporated.

"Frank, are you all right?"

I looked down at Sandy and said, "Oh sure, I'm fine. Just thinking. That's all."

Sandy smiled. "I'm looking forward to seeing you in that boardroom later. Don't worry. People are in your corner. You are going to be a great lieutenant." With that, Sandy excused herself as she carried a large pile of papers to the file/copier room.

After a quick stop in the restroom to make sure my uniform was sharp, I returned to the boardroom. Just like last time, Conrad Zuse was setting up the room for the audio/visual presentation.

Chapter 15: New Officer Orientation Winds Down

"Hi, Conrad," I said.

"Hey, Lieutenant. Today's the big day!"

"Guess so. Any insight into what the fire chief has in store?" I asked.

"Not a clue, but I assure you, you'll enjoy it."

"Thanks."

The Three Musketeers, Reunited

I watched him put the finishing touches on his work, and as he left, Pete and Maggie entered the room. Both looked sharp in their clean, pressed uniforms. Quite a contrast to the last time I'd seen them in the restaurant. Just then, our eyes met. Pete raised his hand and smiled. Maggie turned toward me with a big smile on her face.

"Great to see you. Thanks for all the help during the interviews," she said, giving me a big bear hug.

"No problem," I grunted, as she squeezed the air out of my lungs.

Pete, standing behind her, shook my hand and said, "Me too. I wish we could work in the same firehouse. But I guess that would mean one of us wouldn't get promoted today."

At that, we laughed. They put down their stuff next to the chairs bearing their nameplates. "Wow, looks like one more day of the three musketeers," Pete said, laughing.

He was right. The three of us were sitting together again.

As other groups entered the room, we mingled among them, laughing and comparing notes. Everyone had found the process to be more in-depth than expected. It surely was a lot more comprehensive than handing us a badge, a radio, and wishing us luck. Then, as the clock struck 3:00, I heard from behind me, "Ladies and gentlemen, thank you for being so prompt."

It was the voice of the fire chief. "If you will take your seats, we'll get started. I don't want to waste your time."

He took out a memory stick, inserted it into the computer, and a PowerPoint program flashed up on the screen. With a few more keystrokes, the fire chief was ready to begin and we were in our chairs ready for whatever he had in store.

"Let me begin by saying what a pleasure it has been to observe each of you in your journeys for promotion to company officer. I had certain expectations at the beginning of the process, which each of you far exceeded. Thank you. This process is not so much about completing a set of pre-designated events as it is the beginning of a journey I like to call 'enlightenment.' The very root of the word means to 'remove the dimness or blindness from one's eyes or heart.' When you were told you would be attending the new officer orientation, I am sure you had some reservations, even doubts. During the process, I saw your boundaries expand and your reservations reduced.

"Each of you has embraced this program, opening your eyes and minds to the wonders out there for you to discover. I have received reports of acting officers performing above their positions in the highest traditions of the fire service. I have also received reports of interviews that went well beyond the scope of what you were tasked to accomplish. So before we begin to find out what you discovered about your organization, let me ask if you have any questions."

We looked at each other quizzically, then back to the fire chief.

"Seeing none, let's begin. On your first day I asked you to set aside the red, blue, and green folders and place the purple one in front of you. It had only three pages. The first page showed the Five Pillars of Service: People, Service, Quality, Finance, and Growth. The second page listed the Nine Principles. And on the third appeared the Healthcare Flywheel, tying together the pillars and principles.

"Now let's talk about how these pages impact how our department does business. I'd like each of you to give me one point, and one point only. This way, each of us will be able to participate in the discussion."

He began with the person at the far end of the table from me. It was as if each of us had been taught by the same teacher. The discussion items listed by people started with the center of the Healthcare Flywheel—Purpose, Worthwhile Work, and Making a Difference.

Then began the list of the Prescriptive To-Dos—Commit to Excellence, Measure the Important Things, Build a Culture Around Service, Create and Develop Leaders, Focus on Employee Satisfaction, Build Individual Accountability, Align Behaviors with Goals and Values, Communicate at All Levels, and Recognize and Reward Success.

"Do you understand how each of these fit into the operation of our organization?" He paused for a second. "Do you understand whose responsibility it is to create the culture here?"

Maggie's hand shot up.

"Ms. Winters?" the fire chief acknowledged.

"I understand it's everyone's responsibility. But who teaches the firefighters what the culture should be? Our parents taught us about our family cultures, and our aunts and uncles showed us how we should act in family situations, but what about this environment?" she asked.

Leading the Way

"You bring up an excellent point, Lieutenant. Can I call you that?"

Her face beamed. "Of course, I gotta get used to it sometime. You might as well be the first. You *are* the fire chief!" Maggie answered enthusiastically.

"Thank you for your permission, Ms. Winters. Let me explain. First, understand that we are developing our culture today after having studied this department from a number of angles. We found that getting our older members who are more advanced in rank, like the captains and chiefs, to change is a hard thing to do. It's like telling your grandparents that the hottest new music is the same as what they listened to. I know that my grandparents thought Benny Goodman and Louis Armstrong were 'it.' I thought that way about the Beatles, the Eagles, and Boston. But my grandparents said that 'real' performers don't need names like bugs, birds, and cities. I guess that's a perfect example of a generation gap.

"This same gap exists within our organization. *Some* of our older members will innovate, adapt, and overcome obstacles, but others will not. So instead of fighting the established culture of these individuals, we thought if we started with your group, trained you into the new cultural norm, you will instill these principles into the next generation. You will be the moms and pops of the organization. When our more senior personnel leave through retirement or attrition, our new culture will have become ingrained for their replacements."

Maggie asked, "So what you are saying is we're the cutting edge of this new culture. We will create it for our future, but we may not see the fruits for a few years—just like a seed that is planted and takes a while to germinate, grow, and flower?"

She hit that one for a home run. Boy, was I proud to be a part of this.

"Exactly. And since this is the case, I know I will need to spend additional time assisting in the creation and development of you, our leaders, than I normally would. Each of you will need help in staying motivated until the culture is firmly established. Even if we face a whirlwind of resistance, working together we can overcome any obstacle. You will recall all the leaders who spoke on your first day of orientation are as committed to this as I am. You have administration's entire support."

The fire chief answered our questions for about 30 minutes and wrapped up his comments in short order. You would have thought he choreographed the entire meeting as it stayed so close to schedule. At 3:45, he told us we had about 30 minutes to talk, walk around, and relax before the ceremonies got underway. Maggie, Pete, and I went out into the courtyard and sat down at one of the tables. We talked about our lives, our families, and our interests. As a matter of fact, I found out I had made some new friends whom I could ask for assistance as a new officer. The three of us shared a lot in common.

I glanced down at my watch: 4:13 p.m. "Hey, we better get in there. The fire chief said 30 minutes, and you know what kind of schedule he keeps."

Chapter 15: New Officer Orientation Winds Down

"Boy do I…wish everyone were as prompt," Pete said, laughing.

We got to our seats just in time, as the fire chief walked in precisely at 4:15 by the clock above the door.

"Hope you had a good break. Now let's continue. In front of you there's an envelope with your name on it. There are several things inside, with the first being an evaluation of the new officer orientation process. I ask that you be completely honest with us as to what you think about it. Even the criticism helps us build a better program for tomorrow. I will ask you to fill that out in the next few minutes and leave it in the envelope in your packet. Make sure to seal the envelope and leave it in place on the table. This is totally anonymous.

"After that, I'd like each of you to make recommendations for the next new officer orientation program. We've found that each of you learns at different rates, and we want to make it possible for everyone to be successful. You were handpicked for this orientation. But the next time, it will be for all eligible personnel. This item you can send back through the inter-departmental mail. But please get those back within the week. Anything else you find in the envelope is for you to take home. You will have until 4:45 to finish. Then the boardroom needs to be cleared and prepared for the promotion ceremony. During that time I'd like to invite you and your families into my conference room for a small reception.

"Lastly, I'd like to personally congratulate you on your dedication to this organization and to the community we protect. Without your efforts, we would not have the support of the public nor the confidence they show us by allowing us into their homes and businesses. Thank you."

After the fire chief shook each person's hand with a personal comment of congratulations, he left the room. Immediately, we were all looking around as if to figure out what to do next. Then Pete said, "We'd better get this eval done. Ain't got much time left."

He was right. I looked at the clock on the wall. 4:31 p.m. Fourteen minutes. Not much time indeed.

I opened the envelope and took out the contents. Inside were the two evaluations the fire chief had told us about, an envelope for the anonymous questionnaire, and some other items as well. We found a gift certificate to one of the nicer restaurants in town. The certificate included a dinner for two and a bottle of wine or beverage of our choice. In addition, there was a pen engraved with the department logo and the words New Officer Orientation—Class 01. Also included was a shift calendar, color-coded by specific shift dates, and a letter from the fire chief congratulating us on completion of the program.

I completed the orientation evaluation—including the good, the bad, and the ugly—and was walking out of the room just as Conrad Zuse entered to set up for the next event.

A First-Class Reception

I turned on my cell phone to call Lexi, who, I learned, had just pulled into the parking lot. I told her about the reception and asked her to meet me in the front atrium. She looked terrific. It must have been a new dress, or else I was just really glad to see her—perhaps a little of both. We hugged and I told her what to expect. She smiled and indicated for me to lead the way.

As we approached the fire chief's reception, my hands became sweaty and I told Lexi I was nervous. She said soothingly, "Relax, Frank. You deserve this. Have fun."

She was right—not everyone gets such an opportunity. And besides, I worked hard to be the best paramedic I could be. Just like Maggie worked hard at being "hands-down" the best engineer I had ever seen. I decided right then that the information we had been given was a gift—the gift of excellence in the emergency services. Wow. Nothing could stop us now.

As we entered the conference room, I noticed it had been transformed to a reception area. The table that had been in the center was moved to one side and covered with a linen tablecloth. On it sat a wide assortment of hors d'oeuvres and champagne glasses. This was strange,

Chapter 15: New Officer Orientation Winds Down

since we had a departmental policy dictating no alcoholic intake while in uniform.

The fire chief welcomed us as we entered the door. He was positioned first in a receiving line made up of the members of the Fire Board. Extending his hand, he said, "Congratulations, Lieutenant Benjamin. I look forward to working with you. This must be your lovely wife, Lexi. It is indeed a pleasure to make your acquaintance. I hope you enjoy the evening." He turned to the next person in the receiving line. "Let me introduce the president of our board, Mrs. Roberta Pike."

She shook our hands and welcomed us, offering a congratulatory remark.

After we got to the end of the line, Lexi grabbed my arm. "Did you see that the fire chief was so friendly and knew my name?"

He had definitely done his homework. As I watched the rest of the group file into the reception, he repeated the same actions with differing comments each time. He addressed each spouse by name. He really made an impression on us by demonstrating just how important a person's name is to him or her and to their families.

Not long after the last person entered the room, a group of men and women in white waistcoats and black slacks entered. They proceeded to the conference table and began filling trays with food and beverages. As soon as their trays were full, they circulated among us. It wasn't long before the fire chief addressed the crowd.

"Ladies and gentlemen, I'd like to welcome you to tonight's festivities and offer a toast. So if you'll raise your glasses…"

He hesitated just long enough to scan the room to see who had drinks and who didn't. As soon as the last person held up a glass, the fire chief began again. "Let's toast: To Class 01, the first class of the first class. We look forward to excellence from you in your journeys and offer simply to assist you in making the success of this organization your success as well. Thank you for participating, good luck, and Godspeed." With that, he sipped the contents of his glass, as we all did.

The reception went on for another 30 minutes. I was able to introduce Lexi to the other members of the group, including Maggie and Pete, and they in turn introduced their families. When Lexi suggested to Maggie and Pete that we should all sit together if the opportunity presented itself, it was a plan quickly agreed upon.

The Banquet

As we re-entered the boardroom, we hardly recognized it. The lights in the audience section were dimmed, and the chairs were replaced with round tables that seated eight. The tables held place settings, cloth napkins, a centerpiece, and a brightly lit candle. At each place setting, there was a copy of the program in the center of the plate and a rose or carnation. Later, we would find out that the roses were for the spouses, and the carnations were for each of the new officers. From the ceiling hung what looked like icicles made from strings of white lights.

The board table we had been sitting at earlier had been moved further back so that the platform looked like a stage. At this table, the board members and the fire chief were to have dinner. It was set in similar fashion to each of the round tables.

As we were looking about the room, the fire chief said, "Ladies and gentlemen, welcome to the reception banquet honoring Class 01 of the Officer Development Program. I invite each of you to take seats where you like. Dinner will be served shortly with a ceremony to follow. Enjoy your meals."

Maggie, Pete, and I, along with our spouses, sat at a table furthest away from the front of the room. The meal, which was fantastic, was served by the crew in the white jackets we had seen earlier. Amazingly, the conversation wasn't about the events of the evening, but instead was focused on getting to know one another.

Just as the last person at our table finished the meal, the wait staff appeared to take away the dishes. Moments later, the tinkling of a spoon against a water glass drew our attention to the fire chief. He introduced everyone at the head table, starting with the president of the board on down to the chief officers in attendance. The president made a few comments and returned to her seat. Then the fire chief began his address.

The Fire Chief Inspires

"Good evening, ladies and gentlemen. We are gathered here to recognize the contributions of the men and women of this department who are being honored tonight by promotion. We are certainly proud of their accomplishments and dedication to our organization and to the community we serve. Thanks go out to each of you."

Applause filled the room.

"However, as fire chief and with the permission of the board, I will make just a few short comments.

"History teaches that leadership is fleeting. As difficult as it is to get to the top, it can be more difficult to stay there. National and global competitors want what we have and are determined to get it. As gratifying as the numbers are, complacency is dangerous."

He paused briefly before continuing. "While we work as a government agency, we work for the people of this community. And they deserve the best we can provide. At one time, a private company did what we do. That's how it all began! 'Fire marks' on structures designated who paid for insurance and who didn't. It wasn't as effective as today's service, but it was outside of that provided by government. And without vigilance on our part to keep costs low and service quality high, those days could certainly return.

"But we are not here to challenge you with a history lesson. We're here to honor your accomplishments and to honor you. Each of you has been tested not only by the department, but by circumstances as well, which were often demanding and challenging. But you survived and became better firefighters for it.

"You have taken the second step in leadership. The first was when you helped your supervisor manage the day-to-day operations a little more smoothly. You were leaders who managed not only your own attitudes, but contributed to the advancement of the department through additional training and certification. Not one of you came this far without great sacrifice.

"Let me tell you a story about your journeys. During the story, I want each of you to imagine you are a Labrador retriever."

Everyone looked at one another and smiled.

"And as such you love to play, swim, wag your tail, and get all the love and affection you can possibly handle—sometimes more than your human friend can give. When your human friend picked you up for the very first time, your tail wagged incessantly. Your tongue licked the face of what would turn out to be your best friend. And you were determined to do whatever you could for that person.

"As luck would have it, your friend loved to throw the ball for you and let you bring it back over and over. Neither of you ever tired of doing that. You could trust your friend to play with you, feed you, and provide a soft place to sleep. You would do anything for that person. And then one day while you were playing, your friend introduced you to something new. Your toy sailed into the pond. Glancing towards the pond, you saw ducks swimming, and the water appeared cool and smooth. Lilies floated effortlessly on the surface. All was right with the pond. Until…"

Pausing, the fire chief took a deep breath, "…you jumped in, causing a commotion. Splash! No longer smooth, the water rippled out from you in large circles. The older ducks started squawking and flapping their wings. Angrily, they attacked, scooting towards you, pecking and screeching. Meanwhile, ducklings surfing the waves were squealing with glee at the new-found adventure. What had you done? Everything was okay until you vaulted into the pond. Why were the ducks so upset? The ball had skipped across the water and quietly come to rest. What happened?

"You kept on swimming out to the ball, your eyes following each movement and your tail acting as a rudder. After a few feet, the ripples that caused such a commotion faded away. Now the only ripples were those made by the path you forged as you swam towards the ball, but

Chapter 15: New Officer Orientation Winds Down

these didn't bother the ducks. They were still squawking, but not as loudly. Why?

"As you captured your ball and made for the shore, the ripples streamed out from around your body. Your eyes were now focused on the prize—your human friend waiting on shore, encouraging you to come back with the ball. As you reached land and waded out, the ripples didn't seem so big. *Why?* you wondered. Placing the ball in your human friend's hand, you shook your body from stem to stern to rid your coat of the excess water. Some of the drops hit the surface of the pond and sent their own ripples out.

"Your human friend petted you on the head and told you that you did a great job.

"I think you have a good idea of the picture I am trying to paint. You, as the Labrador, exhibited certain traits—just like you as humans did for these promotions. You were excited, challenged, and looking forward to the new endeavors that would come your way. When you jumped in the pond for the very first time, the old timers squawked about 'their day' and 'we don't need change.' But changes come anyway, whether we want them or not.

"The old timers won't tell you that the same thing happened when they became new officers, except they were the ducks in the smooth pond. They weren't threatened by the dog as long as it was on the shore. And they didn't know the only thing the dog wanted was to please the human friend when it entered the water in pursuit of the ball. So they squawked when their pond changed with ripples set off by the dog. The ripples, ladies and gentlemen, are the changes happening all around us today.

"While I have been tasked with giving you a pep talk, I prefer to challenge you with an understanding of your role. Remember that every action you take—big or small, good or bad—causes change, and the ripples go out from there. You decide what kind of impact you are going to have on this pond of ours. It's the only one we have, and it's up to you to take care of it.

"Some will say to you that we should never lose a firefighter. I wish this were possible, but many great firefighters have heroically made the ultimate sacrifice when they met the unexpected. Selflessness, bravery, and honor run through your veins.

"Ripples of change—we have them with new firefighting tactics and how we apply technology. We know this. But who we are, where we come from, and most importantly, the values we uphold—these are eternal. They are our anchor and the source of our strength as firefighters. We must never permit the intermittent ripple of self-doubt or the ever-changing currents of the rivers of fashion that flow past us to erode that core, or even to introduce a crack in our characters. Remember, we are like the loveable Labrador retriever—constant, ever-ready, and loyal.

"When we stand up for the pinning of the badge of office, we should also stand up with pride, reaffirming our values and the ways they define our firefighting culture. Firefighters must always respect these values and live by them. New standards, new codes, new rules, and improved supervision will change firefighters' behaviors. However, the honor and bravery of firefighters, which has guided our culture so well, are our sources of pride and inspiration. We can hold our heads high.

"Not forged in a day, our spirit has been more than a thousand years in the making. We stand today where our forefathers stood, all together, vowing to make a difference, vowing to be better men and women, better firefighters.

"Our focused efforts, hard work, and training will reduce injuries and deaths. But eliminating all risks is impossible. Doing brave and heroic actions involves danger. We are firefighters who accept the risks because the rewards of our work are so great, and because we have decided to live our values. We will always be putting others' welfare ahead of our own.

"We celebrate the lives of those who fall, because we know every possible safety tool and every piece of relevant training was applied and practiced. We celebrate their lives because we know how hard they worked to ensure their own safety and ours. We celebrate them because they were firefighters.

Chapter 15: New Officer Orientation Winds Down

"Our motto is 'Semper Vigilante': 'ever watchful.' 'Semper Vigilante' of our charges, our citizens, and then ourselves. Every person in this room understands there are things we cannot change. We understand there are things we can and will change…and we know the difference. I know you will protect our values.

"So like our pal the Labrador retriever, when you leave to return to your pond, be aware of the impact you have on the smallest and largest. Watch for those ducks who will try to dissuade you from your work. Watch to see that the ripples you leave are for the good of your brothers and sisters and of the communities you protect. You do make a difference. And lastly, remember there are rewards for the Labradors who retrieve the ball."

Presentation of the Badges

With that, the fire chief relinquished the podium to the president of the board. She called the name of each officer candidate, who stood up, as did his or her spouse. Then all the chief officers shook the hands of the candidates as they went through the line. The fire chief was last. He presented the badge of office and congratulations, handing the badge not to the recipient, but to the spouse to pin it on. Before they could walk away, the fire chief presented collar pins to the new officers, saying, "Good luck."

It was an emotionally moving evening. As the parade of candidates went through the line, families took pictures and shed a tear or two. Lexi sat next to me with her hand on my arm. When they called my name, I felt her squeeze just a little harder as if to say, "You did it."

When the fire chief handed Lexi my badge, she bent closer to pin it on and whispered in my ear, "I am so proud of you…I love you."

Awash with thoughts and emotions, her words made the evening perfect. We went back to the table where Pete and Maggie were waiting for their moments.

"Well," said Maggie, "what did she whisper in your ear?"

I must have blushed 14 shades of red. "I'm not at liberty to say…"

The table broke out in laughter as Maggie rolled her eyes.

"Guess he has the gift of gab."

We all laughed and watched the rest of the new officers get their badges.

After the ceremonies, Maggie, Pete, and I decided we should take everyone out to celebrate. Lexi and I told them we would meet them and headed towards the parking lot. Before we reached the door, Chief Black stopped us.

"Congratulations, Lieutenant," she said.

"Thank you, Chief. Can I introduce my wife, Lexi?"

"It's nice to meet you, Lexi. Lieutenant, may I have a moment?"

"Sure," I responded.

"When I started in the fire service, a mentor of mine informed me of a little tradition. The tradition was simple," she said as she pulled out a worn index card.

On the card was printed, "Attitude Is Everything." Before handing it to me, she recited its contents.

ATTITUDE IS EVERYTHING

Be careful, however. Attitude cannot substitute for experience, skill, or your own growth and aspirations. Your **ATTITUDE** can change the organization one small step at a time. It allows you to control how you feel about anything and everything. You can't always control circumstances. But you can be in control of your attitude, which can make the difference. When the game is on the line, coaches want to get the ball in the hands of their best player. And that player is the one who combines the talent, skill, and attitude to make it happen. Be a go-to player.

Chapter 15: New Officer Orientation Winds Down

She continued, "With this card I give you a token of my confidence in your ability and commitment. Someday you will find an individual who has the same characteristics I see in you today."

She then reached in her pocket, and, without even looking, placed something into my hand and closed my fist around it. "These were given to me by my dad when I became a lieutenant. He got them from his chief. So wear these with pride and pass them on to someone you feel deserves these as you deserve them today. You'll know when the time comes."

I opened my hand and found a worn pair of bugles. They were collar pins.

I looked up as she turned and walked away. I could have sworn I saw her brush a tear from her eye. I didn't know what to say. Just then, Lexi grabbed me. "Congratulations, Lieutenant. I'm going home with the best and bravest."

With that, she planted a kiss and hug. It was some evening.

EPILOGUE

In Front of the Class

I worked for Chief Black as a paramedic for the next couple of years. She helped me hone my skills as a medic and as a lieutenant. When we met on a regular basis, she reinforced the principles I discovered during the new officer orientation. She showed me how important the hub of the Healthcare Flywheel is: Purpose, Worthwhile Work, and Making a Difference. I began implementing the flywheel concept within my fire company from day one. It worked just as well for us as it did for the hospitals for which it was originally designed.

My fire company went from receiving the most complaints and having the greatest personal leave usage to one into which people requested to transfer. It wasn't long before I received a call from the fire chief.

"Lieutenant Benjamin, would you be interested in working on the next new officer orientation program?" he asked.

Wow, I thought to myself, *what an honor. I'd be working with Chief Black and Captain Storm as well as some of the most respected people in the department.* "Sure, Chief, anything I can do to help."

"Good, can you meet with Chief Black in the morning? You'll be temporarily assigned to Admin while the program is underway."

With that he got another call and had to disconnect.

The next morning I met with Chief Black who showed me how the program was put together. We worked on some new ideas, and she asked me to be ready to present the EMS portion. Since public speaking was not my forte, I was a little apprehensive about the presentation part. We worked on the program for about a week until I thought I was ready, and Chief Black agreed. She assured me I would do just fine.

The day came for the new officer orientation, and I was a nervous wreck. But as the fire chief went through his presentation just like last time, I could feel my nervousness waning. Before I realized it, the fire chief was calling me to the podium. Chief Black squeezed my arm, saying, "You can do this. I have confidence in you."

I gave my presentation about the EMS component of the fire service. There weren't that many questions at the end, but I remembered not asking many when my class sat in those seats. It had a much different feel from this side of the table, however. After I finished the presentation, the fire chief gave the class a quick break.

"Good job, Lieutenant. I look forward to working with you more often."

"Thanks, Chief," was about all I could get out.

I needed some water. Although I was still reeling from the presentation, I felt good about it. While at the drinking fountain, Chief Black came up to me. She told me what a good job I'd done as I wiped a drop of water from my chin. I was pleased that both she and the fire chief felt I'd presented the EMS component well. I knew I'd sleep great that night.

The next day, Chief Black and I would be meeting with two of the candidates who were both paramedics. I looked forward to reviewing my notes on what I learned when I went through orientation.

When we met with the candidates, I showed them the Healthcare Flywheel and so began their journeys of discovery. I knew it wouldn't be easy, but if they took this material to heart, they could turn around the operations of the companies they would be taking over. We worked with them until the night of the badge presentation.

Epilogue

New Officers Celebrate

I arrived early to make sure I was prepared and could represent the EMS Department well. Everything was in its proper place and order. All I had to do now was enjoy the show, even though I wouldn't get to share this one with Lexi. She wasn't able to attend since she had work commitments. People began arriving. They looked nervous. *Did I look that way when I went through the ceremony?* I wondered. After the reception, everyone went to the boardroom and took their seats. I was positioned between the fire chief, who hadn't arrived yet, and Chief Black. I hadn't seen her yet tonight and wished I'd called to see if she needed anything before the ceremonies.

The fire chief came in and went to the podium. He welcomed everyone, and after a few pleasantries, we all began to eat. As the waiter delivered my meal, I saw Chief Black and the fire chief talking. He shook her hand and put his arm around her back as he shepherded her to her place.

I stood up as she arrived at the table and waited until she was seated. "Hope everything's okay," I stammered.

"Just fine. Now eat and I'll talk to you later," she whispered.

The presentation went off like clockwork. The new officers were congratulated, badges were given out as spouses cried, took pictures, and fawned over their new officers. The fire chief had changed his presentation a little, and it held more impact. At one point I thought I was about to tear up during his presentation, but somehow held myself in check. If Lexi had been there, she'd have kept me on my game. She would smile and give me "the look" when I came close to losing it. Boy, I could really use her support right then.

Just as the fire chief was about to wrap up the evening, he said he had one more thing to do. He called Chief Black and the president of the board to the podium.

"Over the past few years, Chief Black has been the EMS division chief tasked with creating the award-winning EMS program we enjoy today. This has not gone unnoticed. A few short months ago, I received a telephone call from the mayor of Washington, D.C., and the Speaker of the House of Representatives. They were inquiring about our department's dramatic drop in turnover and the people who made it happen. I told them what a very special person we have in Chief Elle Black.

"I had been grooming Chief Black to be my successor; we've been meeting regularly. She and I developed a mentoring program with her serving as my first mentee, per se. As such, it gives me heartache to announce that Chief Black will be leaving us effective the first of the month. This evening she accepted the position of fire chief for the District of Columbia Fire Department—the one that protects the President of the United States."

It was as if the air had been sucked out of the room. Not a sound or movement. Everyone sat in stunned silence. My mentor was leaving, and she hadn't said a word about it.

"I know that this is sudden, but I would like to honor Chief Black for her dedicated service to our organization. This is a time for celebration. She will be the first female fire chief in the District's history. And she'll have her hands full guiding a department with almost as long a tradition as the United States itself."

The fire chief reached under the podium and pulled out a large rectangular box. He opened it slowly, as if the contents would jump out.

Chief Black stood up next to him. "I know you told me not to do anything," the fire chief said. "But you have left a lasting impression on this department. We will never want for excellence again, as you have shown our team how to develop it. That is your legacy here. Thank you."

With that, he handed her the plaque, hugged her tightly, and exited the stage. The fire chief had never handed over anything so fast. Working so closely with the fire chief and Chief Black, we had built a rapport, and I knew he was simply trying to hold it together.

The president of the board took over from there. "The plaque reads, 'In honor of Elle Black, on behalf of the entire team, please accept this token of our appreciation for your outstanding leadership.'"

Epilogue

Gazing over her shoulder, I could see the face of the plaque. What the audience couldn't see below the engraving was an enamel circle with an etching, in full color, of the Healthcare Flywheel. I looked up at Chief Black just as she was about to speak. A tear was rolling down her cheek.

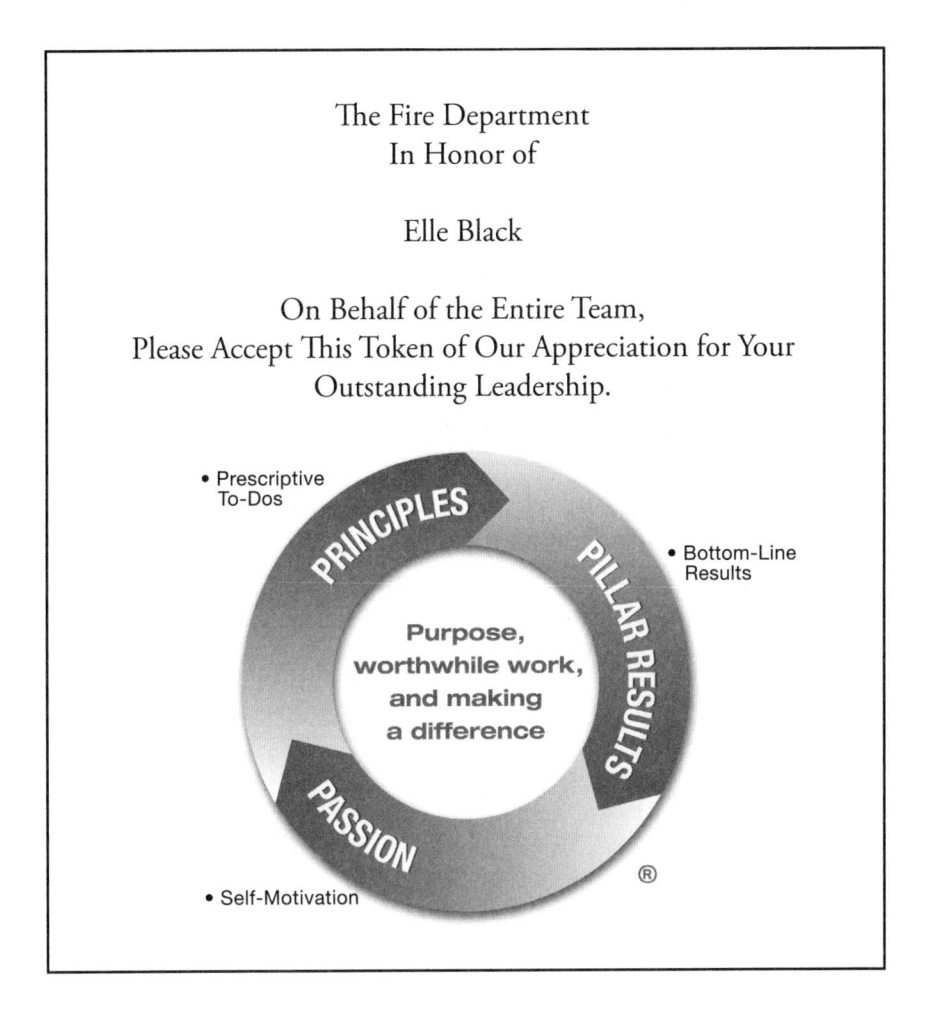

The Fire Department
In Honor of

Elle Black

On Behalf of the Entire Team,
Please Accept This Token of Our Appreciation for Your
Outstanding Leadership.

- Prescriptive To-Dos
- Bottom-Line Results
- Self-Motivation

PRINCIPLES
PILLAR RESULTS
PASSION

Purpose, worthwhile work, and making a difference

"Thank you. I could not have done this without the support and motivation of each of you. I hope you can find your purpose, worthwhile work, and are able to make a difference every day."

With that, she sank into her chair. The room broke out in a standing ovation. The fire chief was applauding her, as was the board and every chief officer at the head table. It was several minutes before the applause died down enough for the fire chief to get a word in. I was applauding on the outside, yet inside I felt totally deflated. I wasn't prepared for this, and my thoughts were in turmoil. What a fantastic opportunity for Chief Black, but…I was losing my mentor, my foundation.

The chief continued, "Chief Black accepted this position only moments before we began tonight's ceremonies. I wouldn't have it any other way. She'll be leaving us to assist another community in reaching new heights as soon as possible.

"Captain Benjamin, would you please stand?" the fire chief said. Confused, I slowly rose to my feet. *Captain? He must be caught up in the moment. He must mean Lieutenant*, I thought.

"Chief Black has already trained her replacement. Effective the first of the month, Captain Frank Benjamin will be heading up our EMS Division."

The room erupted with whistles, back-slapping, high fives, and all-around pandemonium. I stood there in shock. I didn't know what to say. I felt like my jaw was resting on the floor and my heart was blown apart. Before I could say anything, Chief Black was congratulating me with tear-filled eyes, wishing me luck.

ACKNOWLEDGMENTS

The real Frank Benjamin continues to be an inspiration to me. I thank him for being the example of extraordinary service that he is and for allowing me to share his story.

This book is the result of a team effort, not only during the time it took to put these ideas down on paper but throughout my career and the things I learned along the way. To name each would be simply impossible. The team at Fire Starter Publishing I count as more than colleagues. Thanks to Quint Studer for believing in this book and to Bekki Kennedy for her assistance and graceful judgment in the publishing of a work as personal as a book. What you are holding in your hand would not be possible without the design and proofing work of the team at DeHart & Company. Before the manuscript made it to Bekki's desk, Rick Outzen challenged the perceptions and made some improvements that made this book applicable to more than just firefighters or paramedics.

So many friends have inspired, instructed, and encouraged me over the years. Being a member of great fire service organizations has added tremendously to my personal as well as my professional life. There are too many to mention by name, but you know who you are. Please know that I am truly grateful.

But, more than anyone else, I need to thank the real inspiration for this story: Linda—my wife, my companion, my best friend, my biggest supporter. She reviewed countless editions of the story, suggested changes (we all know what *suggested* means), and made this a story about success in bringing excellence into an organization. I used to think those who wrote that kind of stuff were crazy. I didn't realize how true those thoughts were. Linda has made a tremendous difference in my life and my career and nothing can compare to the true gratefulness I have for her generous spirit and her willingness to become my wife.

And finally, to the many individuals—some of whom I've met and others whom I've only heard about—who live in the spirit of pursuing excellence daily and making life fuller and richer for others. I tip my hat and hope you continue to change the world—one person at a time.

RESOURCES

Accelerate the momentum of your Healthcare Flywheel®.
Access additional resources at www.studergroup.com/FrontlineHeroes.

STUDER GROUP COACHING:

Studer Group® coaches hospitals and healthcare systems providing detailed framework and practical how-tos that create change. Studer Group coaches work side-by-side establishing, accelerating, and hardwiring the necessary changes to create a culture of excellence. In our work, Studer Group has identified a core of three critical elements that must be in place for great organizational performance once a commitment is made to the pillar approach to goal setting and the Nine Principles® of Behavior.

Emergency Department Coaching Line
Is a comprehensive approach to improving service and operational efficiency in the Emergency Department. Our team of ED coach experts will partner with you to implement best practices, proven tools, and tactics using our Evidence-Based Leadership℠ approach to improve

results in all five pillars: People, Service, Quality, Finance, and Growth. Key deliverables include decreasing staff turnover, improving employee, physician, and patient satisfaction, decreasing door-to-doctor times, reducing left without being seen rates, increasing upfront cash collections, and increasing patient volumes and revenue.

To learn more about Studer Group coaching, visit www.studergroup.com.

BOOKS: categorized by audience

All Leaders
Hardwiring Excellence—A *BusinessWeek* bestseller, this book is a road map to creating and sustaining a "Culture of Service and Operational Excellence" that drives bottom-line results.
Written by Quint Studer

Results That Last—A *Wall Street Journal* bestseller by Quint Studer that teaches leaders in every industry how to apply his tactics and strategies to their own organizations to build a corporate culture that consistently reaches and exceeds its goals.

Hardwiring Flow: Systems and Processes for Seamless Patient Care—Drs. Thom Mayer and Kirk Jensen delve into one of the most critical issues facing healthcare leaders today: patient flow.

Eat THAT Cookie!: Make Workplace Positivity Pay Off...for Individuals, Teams and Organizations—Written by Liz Jazwiec, RN, this book is funny, inspiring, relatable, and is packed with realistic, down-to-earth tactics leaders can use to infuse positivity into their culture.

"I'm Sorry to Hear That..." Real-Life Responses to Patients' 101 Most Common Complaints About Health Care—When you respond to a patient's complaint, you are responding to the patient's sense of help-

lessness and anxiety. The service recovery scripts offered in this book can help you recover a patient's confidence in you and your organization. Authored by Susan Keane Baker and Leslie Bank.

What's Right in Health Care: 365 Stories of Purpose, Worthwhile Work, and Making a Difference—A collaborative effort of stories from healthcare professionals across the nation. This 742-page book shares a story a day submitted by your friends and colleagues. It is a daily reminder about why we answered this calling and why we stay with it—to serve a purpose, to do worthwhile work, and to make a difference.

101 Answers to Questions Leaders Ask—Written by Quint Studer and Studer Group coaches, offers practical, prescriptive solutions to some of the many questions he's received from healthcare leaders around the country.

Senior Leaders & Physicians
Straight A Leadership—A leadership resource that helps identify obstacles and reveals how to overcome them to execute and lead in 21st century healthcare, written by Quint Studer.

Leadership and Medicine—A book that makes sense of the complex challenges of healthcare and offers a wealth of practical advice to future generations, written by Floyd D. Loop, MD, former chief executive of the Cleveland Clinic (1989-2004).

Engaging Physicians: A Manual to Physician Partnership—A tactical and passionate road map for physician collaboration to generate organizational high performance, written by Stephen C. Beeson, MD.

Physicians
Practicing Excellence: A Physician's Manual to Exceptional Health Care—This book, written by Stephen C. Beeson, MD, is a brilliant

guide to implementing physician leadership and behaviors that will create a high-performance workplace.

Nurse Leaders & Nurses
The Nurse Leader Handbook: The Art and Science of Nurse Leadership—Written by Studer Group senior nursing and physician leaders from across the country, this book is filled with knowledge that provides nurse leaders with a solid foundation for success. It also serves as a reference they can revisit again and again when they have questions or need a quick refresher course in a particular area of the job.

Inspired Nurse and Inspired Journal—By Rich Bluni, RN, helps maintain and recapture the inspiration nurses felt at the start of their journey with action-oriented "spiritual stretches" and stories that illuminate those sacred moments we all experience.

Emergency Department Team
Excellence in the Emergency Department—A book by Stephanie Baker, RN, CEN, MBA, is filled with proven, easy-to-implement, step-by-step instructions that will help you move your Emergency Department forward.

For more information about books and other resources, visit www.firestarterpublishing.com.

ARTICLES:

Quint Studer on 5 Important Issues Facing Healthcare Leaders
The Hospital Review
November 14, 2008

Unlocking the FEAR Foothold
Quint Studer
March 2009

Evidence-Based Leadership
Projects@Work
Quint Studer

How to Achieve and Sustain Excellence
Healthcare Financial Management

To read these articles and view other resources, please visit www.studergroup.com/StraightALeadership.

SOFTWARE SOLUTIONS:

Leader Evaluation ManagerTM: Results Through Focus and Accountability
Studer Group's Leader Evaluation Manager is a web-based application that automates the goal setting and performance review process for all leaders, while ensuring that the performance metrics of individual leaders are aligned with the overall goals of the organization. By using Leader Evaluation Manager, both leaders and their supervisors will clearly understand from the beginning of the year what goals need to be accomplished to achieve a successful annual review, can plan quarterly tasks with completion targets under each goal, and view monthly report cards to manage progress.

To learn more, please visit www.firestarterpublishing.com.

INSTITUTES:

<u>Taking You and Your Organization to the Next Level with Quint Studer</u>
Learn the tools, tactics, and strategies that are needed to Take You and Your Organization to the Next Level at this two-day institute with Quint Studer and Studer Group's coach experts. You will walk away with your passion ignited, and with Evidence-Based Leadership[SM] strategies to create a sustainable culture of excellence.

<u>What's Right in Health Care</u>[SM]
One of the largest healthcare peer-to peer learning conferences in the nation, What's Right in Health Care brings organizations together to share ideas that have been proven to make healthcare better.

To review a listing of Studer Group institutes or to register for an institute, visit www.studergroup.com/institutes.

For information on Continuing Education Credits, visit www.studergroup.com/cmecredits.

Visit www.studergroup.com/FrontlineHeroes to access and download many of the resources, examples, and tools mentioned in *Frontline Heroes*.

ABOUT THE AUTHOR

Author, adventurer, and award-winning firefighter, Kurt Larson has energized hundreds of people. Kurt strives to motivate those around him to better handle the everyday challenges and adventures of life. Kurt has been involved in the fire and emergency services since his first exposure during recruit training in San Diego, California, over 30 years ago. His experience includes positions with both career and volunteer fire departments, advancing to fire chief in both avenues of service. He is a graduate of the National Fire Academy's Executive Fire Officer Program—the Harvard of the fire service—and holds a bachelor's degree in communications engineering as well as a master's degree in education.

Kurt is an innovator and a leader. As a speaker and lecturer, Kurt has presented training and educational programs to organizations around the world. He will take you on a journey that will inspire you to face your own personal and professional fires. Kurt draws analogies between his firefighting adventures and the challenges we face both personally and professionally. He sends the message to excel and live life to its fullest. He challenges the audience to take their own risks and turn dreams into reality. "We all have a fire burning in us to do something spectacular in our lives." As one person wrote, "Kurt is unique, inspiring, and speaks to your heart with a sincere passion for his message."

Not many people have experienced the world as Kurt has. He has seen the world at its best and its worst traveling not only as a firefighter, but as a member of Up with People from the 1980s to 2001. Traveling internationally, he stayed in homes rather than hotels, visiting one on one, learning about people not through a diplomat's eyes, but as a guest in their homes.

He is currently active as an adjunct instructor for the Northwest Florida Fire Academy. Kurt has been honored by being named to Who's Who and was a recipient of the Colorado Governor's Award. In addition to garnering awards for his service to his community, Kurt has shown his leadership in a variety of ways. He was the first certified fire officer in Colorado history and the chairman of the Chamber's Governmental Affairs Committee in Colorado. On an international scale, he is active in the Professional Development Committee as well as the second vice president for the Southeast Association of Fire Chiefs, a division of the International Association of Fire Chiefs.

Kurt has received the rank and title of chief fire officer from the Center for Public Safety Excellence, an international organization that recognizes training, education, and professional contributions of public safety professionals.

Kurt is currently employed by the Florida Institute of Research and Education, a public safety research group, as an analyst and developer. The Institute provides safety-related services for both government and business. Kurt was a member of Leadership Pensacola's best class ever, the class of 2005, and strives to lose that designation by helping future classes be better than the last.

How to Order Additional Copies of

Frontline Heroes
A Story of Saving Lives

Orders may be placed:

Online at:
www.firestarterpublishing.com
www.studergroup.com

By phone at: 866-354-3473

By mail at: Fire Starter Publishing
913 Gulf Breeze Parkway, Suite 6
Gulf Breeze, FL 32561

(Bulk discounts are available.)

Frontline Heroes
is also available online at www.amazon.com.